ANCIENT BYBLOS RECONSIDERED

Part One: THE HISTORICAL REASONS FOR THE CONFUSION CONCERNING GEBEIL/BYBLOS

Part Two: SOME FRESH PROPOSALS FOR FACING THIS PROBLEM

4

PLATE I   PLATE II

FOREWORD

It is not surprising that so much uncertainty has clouded our understanding of the problems related to Gebeil/Byblos when we consider the number of disciplines which are involved in any attempt to examine them more closely. Undoubtedly there will be criticism of my boldness in outlining the problems that exist even today from the point of view of several disciplines in which I am not qualified. But it is to be hoped that, in the interests of both science and sanity, the discussion will centre around the problems themselves rather than on my personal lack of skills.

Many brilliant and energetic young scholars are wasting their time by being encouraged to work on theses related to ancient Egypt, without taking into account that much of its history is not at all secure but interpreted as a chain of assumptions. The sooner we reconsider all these basic assumptions, the sooner we shall be directing our energies towards some truly fruitful goals.

For too long we have followed the law of inertia with regard to these problems. For example, it should have disturbed us all profoundly to see that some of the names that we find on the king-list of Gebeil/Byblos are from monuments which were not even found on that site, but merely assumed to have come from there. No protest about this was ever registered and the names of these rulers are quoted everywhere as certain. Scholars have behaved as though the name of gbl were a unique one, impossible to confuse with any other. But gbl is one of the most common names in the whole of the Near East.

The time has come to look again at our text-book picture of Gebeil/Byblos in the light of the facts alone and to re-assess it radically. It emerges as a much more complex one than any we have been prepared to consider so far.

Alessandra Nibbi

ACKNOWLEDGEMENTS

My thanks must go the Security Authorities of the Arab Republic of Egypt for allowing me to travel extensively in the delta to visit many towns of non-archaeological interest until now which were previously only names on a map for me and others. My thanks are also offered to the Egyptian Antiquities Organization who allowed me to visit archaeological sites in the delta and elsewhere and to the many people within that Organization who helped me to understand the difficulties of conservation on the sites of such a fast-developing area as the delta of Egypt.

Furthermore, my gratitude to the Governor of Ismailia, Dr. Abdul Moneim Emara and his most efficient Public Relations team must be expressed. Mr. Mahmoud Ibrahim, Miss Fatma Mansour and Mr. Mohammed Hassan Ibrahim all helped me to understand the geography of that region and to find the Gebal El Gibali, which has now largely disappeared to make space for cultivation.

Yet again my thanks to the Griffith Institute and the Ashmolean Library must be recorded. The use of these facilities has been of the greatest value to me, as also the help over the years received from Professor John Baines and Dr. Jaromir Málék and his staff of the Topographical Bibliography.

Photographs from the Turin Museum and the Petrie Museum are published by their courtesy.

Nor must I omit to thank Mr. John Connaughton and the Bocardo Press for the practical production of this study.

Alessandra Nibbi
July, 1985.

8

PLATE III

PLATE IV

LIST OF FIGURES

LIST OF PLATES

I.   Statuette of unknown provenance now in the Turin
      Museum, catalogue no. 3036, Inventory no. 5544.
      See Rec. Trav. II, 120.

II.   ibid. Published by courtesy of the Turin Museum.

III. This photograph shows the road which has long since
      cut through the mound of El Gibali. The remainder
      of the mound on the left with the modern obelisk is
      called Gebel Mariam.

IV.   This view of the remaining part of El Gibali is
      taken from the area where the former mound had
      stood, which is now given over to cultivation.

V.   This is a closer view from the land side showing
      the current state of bulldozer excavation in
      February 1982.

VI.   A closer view again of the newly uncovered floor of
      this mound, teeming with pottery. The author's
      photograph is included to show the normal direction
      of the wind, coming from the north.

VII. The remaining part of the mound of Bilbeis when the
      author visited it in the winter of 1979.

VIII. A closer detail of this same area, not far from the
      school building which sits on the only remaining
      part of this important and totally neglected ancient
      mound.

IX.   Another view of the remaining stratification of
      Bilbeis, nearer to the bridge over the modern
      canal.

X.   Vase found in the vicinity of Bilbeis, now in
      University College, London, published by their
      courtesy.

12

PLATE V

PART ONE

THE HISTORICAL REASONS FOR THE CONFUSION CONCERNING GEBEIL/BYBLOS

i) Byblos and the Lebanon.

Several times already[1] I have had occasion to question the relationship between ancient Egypt and the town that we call today Gebeil/Byblos. Upon close examination, the facts do not correspond to the way they are presented in the textbooks where the main link between ancient Egypt and this town is the supposed importation of cedar by ancient Egypt. In Ancient Egypt and Some Eastern Neighbours (1981) I followed Victor Loret[2] in emphasizing that the word $^c\underline{s}$, which is used for ancient Egypt's most valued, resinous and fragrant wood, cannot possibly mean cedar. It is more likely to mean pine and this has been abundant upon Egypt's borders for several millennia, right up to the present day.[3] The scientific evidence has not yet shown that large quantities of cedar were ever used by the ancient Egyptians and there is certainly no evidence at all that they used cedar to build boats. Apart from the fact that all boatbuilders agree that it is a most unsuitable wood for this purpose, the lateral pattern of growth of the Cedar of Lebanon, which is its distinguishing feature, makes it a difficult timber for producing long straight logs which is another traditional argument on this topic.[4] However, juniper wood, which is very similar to cedar in appearance to the naked eye, has been abundant in the northern Sinai from chalcolithic times[5] until now when only a very small scatter of this ancient forest still remains.

The importation of cedar from the Lebanon by ancient Egypt[6] is made even more unlikely by the finding in recent times of cedar pollen in the northern highlands of the Sahara, among the remains of oak and other Mediterranean vegetation, which is known to have been present along much of north Africa during the Late Quaternary wet period lasting probably well into the early dynastic period of Egypt.[7] It is a well-known fact that forests tend to live on even after the rainfall declines, as long as the soil cover remains. Moreover, the text of Meri-ka-re tells us that the mrw-wood, known to be reddish-brown in colour and very probably meaning cedar, came from the west,[8] thus agreeing with a recent and independently-established scientific fact.

All the references from the ancient Egyptian texts referring to the importation of $^{c}\underline{\underline{s}}$-wood by Egypt have until now been interpreted as referring to cedar even though Victor Loret had shown in 1916[9] that the colour of this wood was a very pale yellow, with no grain markings on it.[10] This, together with the fact that we are talking of a highly resinous wood, is most consistent with pine. We know that this tree was prolific in southern Palestine from pre-biblical times until the First World War and that it probably grew quite thickly in the Egyptian delta itself.[11] Egyptologists are now beginning to accept that the delta was, in ancient times, a territory largely foreign and often hostile to the Pharaoh.[12]

It is therefore not only not proved, but not even likely, that Egypt ever received any wood from the Lebanon at all, because all the woods that were used in ancient Egypt can now be shown to have been present either in Egypt itself or along its borders.

As to the repeated assertions by scholars that timber was transported from Gebeil/Byblos to Egypt possibly by the method that is shown on the Khorsabad reliefs[13] with three logs tied overhead from bow to stern, acting as a kind of hogging-truss and four other logs hauled in the water behind the boat, it is simply not possible for this method of transport to have taken place anywhere on any sea. It is quite beyond the realms of possibility that ships could carry such a load on the high seas even on calm water, because the gentlest movement of the waves would shift the weight and the pull of these very heavy logs in the water in unpredictable and uncontrollable directions. Such a form of transport was possible only on an inland water, and even then only during a windless period. We must remember that in the story of Wenamun which until now has been generally accepted as having taken place along the Near Eastern coast, seven logs was the full load for a transport boat,[14] suggesting this method of transport.

It is a well-known fact that the Near Eastern coastline is almost totally devoid of harbours so that the occurrence of a storm could spell disaster very quickly. Moreover, the currents along this coast are known to depend upon prevailing winds from the south-west (see our fig. 1).

In making this point that the Palestinian coast has never produced a maritime people, George Adam Smith in 1894 summarized this situation very succinctly:

"Everyone remembers, from the map, the shape of the east end of the Levant. An almost straight line runs from north to south, with a slight inclination westward. There is no large island off it, and upon it no deep estuary or fully sheltered gulf. North of the headland of Carmel nature has so far assisted man by prompting here a cape, and dropping there an islet, that not a few harbours have been formed which have been, and may again become, historical. When we remember that the ships of antiquity were small,

propelled by oars and easily beached, we
understand how these few advantages were
sufficient to bring forth the greatest maritime
nation of the ancient world - especially with
the help of the mountains behind, which,
pressing closely on the coast, compelled the
population to push seaward for the means of
livelihood.

"South of Carmel the Syrian coast has been
much more strictly drawn. The mountains no
longer come so near to it as to cut up the water
with their roots. But sandhills and cliffs,
from thirty to a hundred feet high, run straight
on to the flat Egyptian delta, without either
promontory or recess. A forward rock at
CAthlit, two curves of a beach at Tanturah,
twice low reefs - at Abu Zaburah and Jaffa - the
faint promise of a dock in the inland basin of
Askalon, with the barred mouths of five or six
small streams - such are all the possibilities
of harbourage on this coast. The rest is merely
a shelf for the casting of wreckage and the
roosting of sea-birds. The currents are
parallel to the coast and come north laden with
sand and Nile-mud, that helps to choke the few
faint estuaries and creeks. It is almost always
a lee-shore; the prevailing winds are from the
south-west."[15]

Thus George Adam Smith rightly concluded that the
Nile has not only created Egypt, but helped to form the
Syrian coast as well. Scientific evidence from the
pollens found in the sea off this coast and analysed by
Martine Rossignol[16] bear witness to this fact.

We must remember that Gebeil/Byblos was even
further north than this coast and thus even more
inaccessible by sea from Egypt. George Adam Smith

arrived at two conclusions resulting from the
indisputable inhospitality of this coastline: no invader
was ever able to disembark an army south of Carmel, till
the country behind the coast was already in his power;
even invaders from Europe found their way into Palestine
by land, either from Egypt or from Asia Minor.

As we shall see, Gebeil/Byblos did not have much of
a harbour at any time in its history, not even after
building the two lateral "arms" on its encircling reefs
(see our fig. 6). This is clear even on the excellent
present-day photographs of this site published by Nina
Jidejian in her book Byblos Through the Ages (1968), pp.
150ff. It is possible that we may have made a mistake in
thinking that this was the biblical city of Gubal,
instead of a more northern city, as we shall see.

ii) The Lebanon (sic) and Djahy in the Egyptian Texts.

The Wörterbuch II, 414 lists rbrn as the Lebanon,
usually written with the article pꜣ and attested from the
New Kingdom. The same volume II, 421 also lists rmnn for
the Lebanon from the Eighteenth Dynasty onwards. Both
names are suggested as having a Semitic provenance.
These entries have long needed closer examination.

As far back as 1858, Heinrich Brugsch[17] had
complained that the name Lebanon had already been
accepted by many Egyptologists without discussion, simply
on the basis that some similar-sounding names were to be
found in the topographical lists of the pharaonic texts.
He very rightly objected to this acceptance and
emphasized that there was no evidence to support it. He
stressed that it was most unlikely to find the name of a
mountain among the lists of defeated peoples, countries
and cities. It was more likely, he said, that this name
referred to some other site much closer to Egypt.

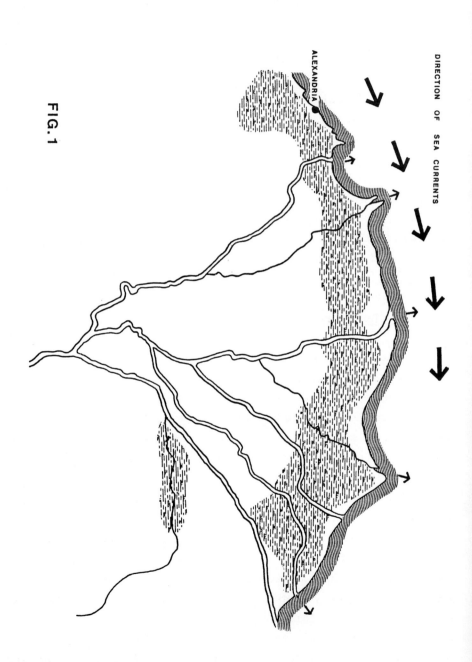

FIG. 1

Brugsch drew attention to the town called Lebonah,[18]
just north of Shiloh in the mountains east of Joppa, as a
possible site for the Egyptian rbrn or rmnn (Judges
21:13 , see our fig. 2).

It should also be noted that the biblical texts
refer to two different cities called Libnah: one is in
Judah and identified as Tell es-Safi (Joshua 10:29ff;
15:42; 21:13, see our fig. 2); the other has been known
to be in northern Sinai (Numbers 33:20-21), but not yet
identified. I believe this must be the Gebel Libni
studied by M. Fourtau early this century[19] and also
marked on our fig. 2. It is interesting to recall in
this context that there is evidence of an extensive
juniper forest in northern Sinai in ancient times.[20]

Most important of all, however, is the presence of
a town of this name in the eastern delta, immediately
south/south-east of Facus, variously written Lebna,
Lobainah, Labna, Labina (see our sketch map fig. 2).[21]
Why, then, should we be looking so far north to explain
this ancient name from the Egyptian records?

Wolfgang Max Müller supported Brugsch[22] in his
complaint about the lack of evidence for the
identification of rbrn and rmnn as the Lebanon and he
stated his belief that we owed this to John Gardner
Wilkinson though he does not quote a specific reference
to this effect. Max Müller suggested that this early,
unsupported interpretation of rmnn as the Lebanon was due
largely to the well-known reliefs of Sethos I at
Karnak,[23] where so-called Asiatics are shown cutting
down trees with their double axes as an illustration of
the text.

We have already referred to recent studies of the
vegetation of ancient Egypt showing that we must take
into account the existence of a thick pine and oak forest

in southern Palestine from pre-biblical times until our own, for which the evidence is indisputable.[24] We must also accept the fact that pine grew in the Egyptian delta, together with other Mediterranean vegetation, probably throughout the whole pharaonic period.[25] The facts are summarized in our figure 2 here.

The argument requiring ᶜš to be understood as cedar, and thus as having to be obtained from the Lebanon, did not enter into the discussion concerning this area until nearly half a century later, as the result of the work of Adolf Erman[26] and Kurt Sethe.[27] Such was the reputation of these scholars that this idea remained entrenched until today, even after the article by Victor Loret in 1916[28] which showed clearly that ᶜš could not be cedar. My own discussion that cedar is of very limited use and that ᶜš very probably meant pine are set out elsewhere,[29] together with references to the pollen evidence showing cedar to have been present in the Saharan highlands in late prehistoric times.

The fundamental assumption that rbrn and rmnn are referring to the Lebanon has never been questioned in recent years either, not even in the important and otherwise thorough discussions of A. H. Gardiner,[30] Wolfgang Helck[31] and Claude Vandersleyen.[32] It is a warning to us all that mere opinion without a shred of proof should have become so firmly fixed a doctrine in our textbooks. The belief that all the Mediterranean timber used in ancient Egypt had to come from the Lebanon, even if it was not cedar, has never been questioned in the last fifty years, in spite of the fact that there was never any evidence to support it. To make matters more complicated, the Lebanon has been linked closely to Gebeil/Byblos,[33] from which city, the Egyptological textbooks tell us, timber was brought (sic) by sea to Egypt. To get some clarity into this picture, we must treat each part of it separately.[34]

A document from Gebel Barkal gives us a clear statement as to where to place rmnn. It refers to the "true $^c\underline{s}$-wood of rmnn" which was cut in Djahy every year (fig 3).[35] We know that pine is the most consistently resinous of all the trees. If $^c\underline{s}$ means pine in this context then it was available either in the Egyptian delta, or, at its most northern location, in southern Palestine (see fig. 2). The text suggests that the seasonal task as well as the return journey could be completed well within twelve months.

The discussion of Djahy[36] so far has not led us to define even an approximate area for it. It is usually understood to mean Palestine/Syria. But this conclusion was arrived at not by any scientific hypothesis, but only on the basis of what it ought to be if the assumed acceptances for the other names linked with it are correct. This does not make for progress. The most comprehensive effort in this respect has been that of Claude Vandersleyen[37] who rightly emphasized in his study that Djahy was a geographical term[38] and not one designating a nation or a state. He quoted passages from Papyrus Anastasi II 1,2 and ibid. IV 6,2 referring to the pharaonic residence which was situated between Djahy and t3 mrj and, according to Alan Gardiner,[39] not far from the waters of Horus. We know these waters to have come from the Nile so that Djahy could not have been very far from the main stream of the Great River.

Vandersleyen's discussion refers to some other documents which give us information about Djahy, including Papyrus Hermitage 1116 A verso.[40] However, the interpretation of this particular passage is based on the assumed and unproved identifications of a number of other place-names and cannot therefore provide us with the firm and conclusive evidence that we need in order to define Djahy. Vandersleyen includes in his discussion other texts where Djahy is linked with Retenu and the

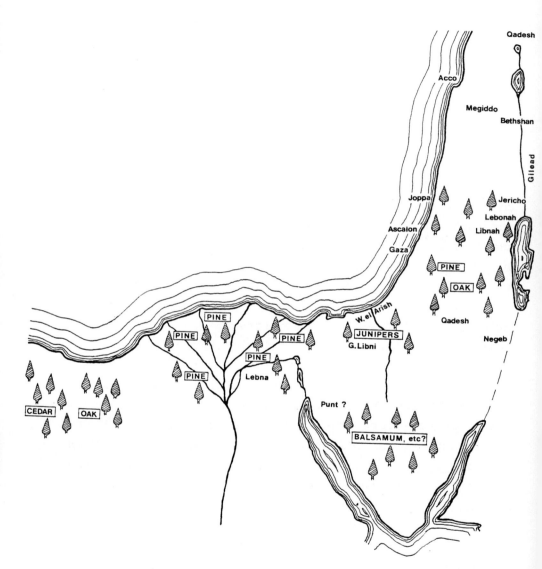

FIG. 2

Euphrates (sic).[41] Thus no matter how secure these identifications appear to be, they are as yet only assumptions. Nor can we arrive at any identification of Djahy by getting any perspectives from the Fenkhu[42] who still remain unidentified and the subject of speculation only.

Although it is not yet clear to us exactly where Djahy was we know it to have been close to the border of Egypt because the Pharaoh had his residence there and also because that was where he prepared his defences against possible attacks from the enemy.[43] It is clear from the text we quoted above (our fig. 3) that while rmnn was certainly a place where timber grew, it was not very far from Egypt, because it was within the area of Djahy.

Agreed as we all are that Djahy was a geographical area, I believe we could understand it better by looking more closely at the meaning of the name itself.

It is possible to accept d3 in the sense of crossing water, according to the Wörterbuch V, 511, while the second part of this name may have been derived from h3j, meaning to descend by water, according to the Wörterbuch II, 472. The combination of these two ideas in one name could be said to summarize the physical nature of the delta region in relation to the Nile proper, where there was only one stream (fig. 4). A name consisting of these two words very clearly conveys a picture of a watery environment in descent to its lowest levels. It conveys the idea of the strange and complex nature of the delta landscape with its many waterways and flooded depressions after leaving the main single stream of the Great River. This single stream was well understood by the dweller along its banks and was quite predictable. But the delta was totally different. Such a complex watery environment was foreign to him.

Furthermore every stream in the northern region could carry the threat of incoming enemies travelling by water. For this reason Djahy was a place where fortifications were built and maintained. The defences in Djahy were always the first thought of the pharaoh in the New Kingdom when told of an imminent attack.

Such a definition of Djahy is not only apt, but acceptable, I believe. It emphasizes for us the graphic reality of the difference in the environment of the delta as seen by the dweller along the Nile proper.

The archaeological record of the delta in recent years is making it easier to accept what I have been stressing for the last decade[44] that the delta of Egypt was not part of the Egyptian kingdom during the pharaonic period. It now seems certain that three at least of the traditional enemies of Egypt, the Nine Bows, had their home in the delta, namely the ḥ3w-nbwt,[45] sḫt-j3m[46] and t3 mḥw,[47] which has never been disputed as to its general location, but only in the detail of its exact extent (see fig. 4). Furthermore, few Egyptologists would dispute the likelihood that the delta may also be the sole location for the tḥnw. If these identifications are accepted from the evidence upon which they are based, and not on the traditional but unfounded assumptions, it is possible that we may find four of the Nine Bows living in the delta during the pharaonic period.

To return to our quotation from Gebel Barkal (fig. 3) telling us that it was in Djahy that the true ꜥš of rmnn was cut each year. It must be stressed that quite independent palaeobotanical studies have established that pine and other Mediterranean trees grew in the delta of Egypt in ancient times.[48] We are still waiting to obtain precise historical dates for these which will only become available in the course of time by comparative studies with neighbouring areas. But the existence of these and other forests is beyond dispute and cannot be ignored.

It is a sad fact that rbrn and rmnn became accepted as the Lebanon very early in our Egyptological studies without proof or the benefit of discussion of any kind. These acceptances became enshrined in the Wörterbuch in the early years and students thereafter inevitably absorbed them without question.

It is an even sadder fact that when I produced scientific proof that oak and pine forests were abundant on Egypt's borders in earlier times so that Egypt did not need to send to the Lebanon for any of its timber, no less a scholar than K. A. Kitchen insisted that this was nonsense, because, as he said, rmnn indubitably meant the Lebanon.[49] A similar argument was put forward by Claude Vandersleyen[50] just as though I had produced no evidence at all for what I had said! Both scholars chose to ignore the indisputable reality of the forests, for which independent proof exists and to contradict me merely by re-iterating the traditional assumptions. Neither felt it to be necessary to question the basis for their belief or to produce any argument to sustain it seriously. I subsequently challenged K. A. Kitchen on this and other assertions of his for which there is no justification.[51]

Either we have, at long last, that delayed fundamental and reasoned discussion with regard to the acceptance of rbrn and rmnn as the Lebanon, if any proof can indeed be produced, or else we set it aside as an error to be forgotten as soon as possible.

iii)   Byblos, Gebal and kbn/kpny: Not Synonymous.

It was F. Chabas who in 1866 first studied the

PLATE VI

PLATE VII

Egyptian name kpny.[52] An earlier form of this word was
recognised by Kurt Sethe in kbn[53] but not until after
Chabas had written his book. The name kpny occurs in
Papyrus Anastasi I which the French scholar was
discussing and it is to the credit of Chabas that his
study and proposed solution of the problem were so very
acceptable to the Egyptologists of his day that it has
hardly been questioned since then. It is to be noted
however that the scholars of his day did not always give
him the credit for the identification of kpny as Gebal or
later Gebeil.

Chabas associated kpny, which he vocalized as
kapuna (French form, kapouna) with the Semitic Gabaon
which he derived from the Biblical Gebal. He believed
that Kapaon and Kabal could be explained by the frequent
"confusion" of the sounds k and q and of p and b when
Semitic words were transcribed into the Egyptian. As to
the l, we know that it did not exist in ancient Egyptian
and was usually substituted by r or n.

However, Chabas did not stop there. Having
satisfied himself that kpny could be equated with the
common Semitic name of Gebal, he went on to say that it
was therefore Gebeil/Byblos, by drawing largely and
literally on the myth of Osiris as it was transmitted to
us by Plutarch[54] and by Lucian in his De Dea Syria.[55]
It is not my purpose here to trace the ancestry of this
particular classical tradition, but merely to draw
attention to the chronological problem in taking this
late myth as evidence in the discussion of the origin of
the name Byblos. Yet it was these two particular sources
which were an essential and integral part of the
discussion of Chabas when he identified kpny as
Byblos.[56] He then confirmed this relationship between
Egypt and Byblos by alluding to the objects with Egyptian
hieroglyphic inscriptions which had already been found at
Gebeil/Byblos with considerable excitement by Ernest
Renan, the first excavator of that site.[57]

The conclusion by Chabas that kpny could only be Gebeil/Byblos was taken up immediately by the leading Egyptologists of that time, including that authoritative scholar Wolfgang Max Müller,[58] albeit with some reservations. These arose from Max Müller's inability to understand how the Egyptian word could have an etymological link with the Semitic Gublu/Gob(a)l in that existing form, a point which has worried few scholars since then. Max Müller could only justify this equivalence by assuming that kbn was an older form of the name in the Semitic context itself, which Egypt had adopted in earlier times.[59] To this day we have no authoritative etymological study of the Semitic root[60] and there can be no doubt that Max Müller was right in saying that there are serious chronological problems in linking gubl- and kbn/kpny very closely.

Another early objection to the conclusion by Chabas was from Raymond Weill, who said in 1908 in a discussion of Sinuhe[61] that if this particular equivalence of place-names were to be accepted, any of the many places called Gebal would do and there was no special reason for it to be Gebeil/Byblos. His view was criticized and rejected by Alan Gardiner in his own commentary on Sinuhe.[62] Nevertheless Weill had made an important point which cannot be overlooked and to which we shall return below.

A fact which must be emphasized from the very outset of any discussion on kbn/kpny is that both forms of the ancient name (if they are indeed one and the same!) are always written with the hill-country determinative and never with a town sign.[63] Only occasionally in very late times, from Wenamun onwards, do we see a town determinative accompanying the hill-country. But even then it is rare. As we shall see below, the ancient Egyptian records never refer to kbn/kpny as a city or a town, which would imply a

physical, social and administrative structure as the
Egyptian town determinative clearly suggests. Nor is it
designated specifically as a temple site, though the
texts, and particularly a statuette now in Turin Museum
(see our Plates I and II)[64] clearly associate Hathor
with this place, as with many others. She probably had a
shrine there at least.

The ancient Egyptians referred to kbn/kpny
essentially as a source for ʿš-wood and as a
boat-building centre, which would naturally have been
situated where the timber was plentiful, as well as near
water. We shall be looking at examples of this in the
following section, and we shall also be asking the
question as to whether the two writings of this name are
certainly referring to the same place. Our immediate
problem here is to consider whether the Egyptian forms of
this name are beyond doubt equivalent to the Greek Byblos
and the Semitic Gebal. The discussion of the Egyptian
name is greatly complicated by the fact that scholars
from the Semitic and Greek philological fields have
accepted it without discussion as equivalent to their
own designation for Gebeil/Byblos. Nor has any scholar
yet faced the possibility that any or all of these names
might not be referring to Gebeil/Byblos at all.

Some years ago Della Vida[65] pointed out that even
a tenuous link between Gubl- and kbn/kpny requires both
words to convey the meaning of a small hill. If Byblos
is an exactly equivalent term, that too should convey
this basic idea. As the Near Eastern area is full of
tells and Gebeil/Byblos is situated upon a coastal
terrace at a height of approximately thirty metres, no
problem is posed on this basis.

No philological difficulties were recognized by G.
J. Thierry in the Semitic or Greek context when he wrote
his note "Gebal, Byblos, Bible-Paper" in 1951,[66]

FIG. 3

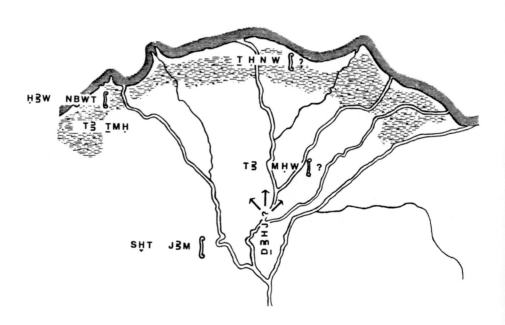

FIG. 4

bringing together all these names to show their close
relationship with the Gubla of the Amarna Letters. He
did not discuss the validity or otherwise of any of the
consonantal changes and quoted Brockelmann's Gundriss I,
199 to affirm the well-known phonetic rule changes of a
to u as in gapnu to gupnu, meaning vine and immu to ummu
meaning mother.

In 1977, a case is built on the equivalence of the
Egyptian kbn/kpny with Byblos by a scholar of the Linear
scripts, Daniel Was.[67] He compares the Egyptian name
with ku-pa-nu and its variations from both Linear A and B
tablets from Knossos and Hagia Triada in Crete.[68] This
is an exciting comparison which may prove right in the
course of time as far as the name itself goes. However
some problems arise when one attempts to relate either of
these names to the place we know today as Gebeil/Byblos.
This basic assumption is not questioned by Was, who also
accepts the derivation of the Greek name of Byblos from the
Semitic forms: Ugaritic gbl, Hebrew g^{e}bal, Babylonian
gubla. Yet this generally accepted view has not been
thoroughly discussed and settled by Semitic and Greek
scholars so far. Pierre Chantraine certainly disputes
such a provenance for the name of Byblos in his
Dictionnaire Etymologique and he emphasizes that this
name is not of Indo-European origin.[69]

As long ago as 1932, in an important study which
has been almost totally neglected, Giacomo Devoto[70]
discussed the root bubl- in the Mediterranean context and
considered the possibility of its being linked with the
common forms publ-/bubl- which he believed were present
in that area in the pre-Indo-European period. He
analysed some of the sound changes which are known to
have occurred in some of the geographical names deriving
from this basic root in the western Mediterranean and he
listed Publisca, Boplo, Popolo, Popli, Poppi, Pupluna
(Populonia). All these particular sites, he believed,

corresponded to the requirement of the Semitic root Gbl-
to refer to a height or a small hill.[71]   But he noted
other place-names where this relationship is not evident
but which appear to be derived from the same root:
Popoli, Popolano, Bubbio, Buggio, Bogliasco, Bogli,
Bobbio.[72]

Devoto found a definite geographical northern
boundary for the names deriving from pupl- and bubl- for
the Italian peninsula, approximately at the level of
Populonia.   Such names, he found, disappeared further
north with very few exceptions.[73]   He suggested the
possibility that the root publ-/bubl- might have come
from a pre-Indo-European word meaning to grow, from which
the meaning of height or elevation was derived.   The name
of byblax survives in southern Italy for a profuse kind
of oleander.[74]

When he came to discuss the name of Byblos, Devoto
found an equally large number of names which seem related
but which, he suggested, may well only be
similar-sounding names bearing no relationship.   He found
this problem to be magnified by the alternating u and i
sounds in the root vowel of the Aegean names.   Moreover,
the fact that such names were to be found in areas as far
removed from each other as Caria and Thrace suggested to
him that they probably preserved a root based in a common
ancestry.   Giving literary sources for the names deriving
from this root Devoto listed from Thrace[75]: a people and
a city, a region and mountains probably in this same
area.   From Caria he listed[76]: a city and a region of
this name, a shepherd, a spring, a mountain and a city
near Miletus, and a daughter of Miletus.   Devoto also
noted such names among the Aegean islands[77] and he
listed also a river in Naxos, a wine probably from Naxos
and the father of Aphrodite.   Devoto concluded that, far
from being able to understand the relationship between
all these names, all that we can say for the present with

any certainty is that their antiquity is attested in the east.[78]

When Emilia Masson analysed this problem in depth in 1967,[79] she offered an authoritative discussion of the difficulties which arise for scholars of Greek if they suppose that the Greek name of Byblos is derived from the Semitic Gubla. She believes that the chief problem lies in the initial consonant because no parallel examples can be found in the Semitic context. Moreover, as Byblos is not an Indo-European name, the rules governing the evolution of certain sound changes in that group of languages cannot be applied here. Emilia Masson reminds us that Byblos as a topographical name for Gebeil appears comparatively late among the classical writers, beginning with Strabo,[80] while the adjective referring to a papyrus rope may already be found in Homer, Odyssey xxi, 391. The words bublos and biblos were in use in the Greek language long before the geographical name of Byblos.

The second great problem that this scholar sees in the establishment of this name is the historical and semantic one in trying to relate the noun bublos to the name of the city. She argues that the Greeks must first have known the papyrus plant which they called by that name and afterwards applied the name to the writing material that was made from it. This scholar quotes evidence[81] to show that the naming of a foreign city or town from a Greek noun is not unheard of, but that it is not a frequent occurrence.

The common assumption among scholars seems to be that the Greek (sic) name of Byblos was derived somehow from the name of the papyrus plant. However, there are difficulties arising from this view. Firstly, no papyrus can possibly have grown in this or any other city situated on a hill because papyrus requires swampy conditions and an unchanging water-level in order to thrive.[82] Nor will papyrus grow along the banks of a river, as for example the one to the south of Gebeil/Byblos, because the water-level of rivers fluctuates seasonally and also because it is flowing water rather than the still swampland required by papyrus. In his studies of papyrus in classical antiquity, this point is not sufficiently emphasized by Naphthali Lewis[83] though he gives us a good account of the papyrus and paper industry in Greek and Roman times.

It has often been suggested that the name of Byblos came to be applied to the Lebanese city because of the great quantities of papyrus writing material which are believed to have been imported into Greece from there. But it is not easy to see why this site should be so closely connected to papyrus at all. This plant cannot have grown there because of the absence of swampland so such a view would require us to see Byblos as a port for the transshipment of cargoes of papyrus writing material.

This too is difficult to accept. Firstly, it seems unlikely that such large quantities of papyrus can have been involved as to override any other more basic commodity that may have been imported into Greece from abroad at that time. Secondly, why should such a large quantity of any foreign product be trans-shipped only from Byblos, and not from other neighbouring ports along that coast such as Tyre and Sidon? Thirdly and most importantly, such a view is almost impossible to accept because we know that the Greeks were settled in the Egyptian delta by the last quarter of the seventh century B.C. with their own port at what was later to become Alexandria.[84] From there they had direct communication and trade with their former homeland. It is in fact from the sixth century B.C. that we begin to have good evidence of a substantial consumption of papyrus in the Greek world though it may well already have been in common use before that time.

Naphthali Lewis believed that in the classical period papyrus was grown and the writing material made mainly in Egypt, even though it was to be found as a decorative motif on early Cretan vases. This belief was no doubt encouraged by the fact that Egypt seemed to be the only producer of good paper at that time. Lewis in fact quotes from a fourth century geographer who said that paper was a thing made nowhere but in Alexandria and its vicinity.

More recently, Peter Warren[85] has offered convincing evidence for the existence of papyrus in the Aegean during the Bronze Age. He has shown beyond all doubt that the detail in the representation of papyrus from Bronze Age sources in the Aegean reflect a direct contact with the growing plant and not merely a secondary contact through imports. Warren illustrates his examples from Thera, Knossos and Phylakopi where the colour on the detail of the paintings reveals that this plant was widely known in the Aegean at that time. There can be no question of the importation merely of papyrus stalks or a rooted plant from one site to another, because papyrus wilts within a matter of hours and becomes totally limp and lifeless within that time.

Yet while conceding the presence of the papyrus plant in the Aegean in the Bronze Age, we must, I believe, accept the statements of the ancient writers that paper-making was primarily an Egyptian craft. We must remember that though several varieties of papyrus are known, it was the cyperus papyrus with the thick triangular stem from which the rolls of writing material were produced and upon which the ancients wrote.

Classical sources tell us that papyrus grew in Egypt in the Sebennytus and Arsinoite nomes, in Sais and in the region of Alexandria, particularly in that arm of

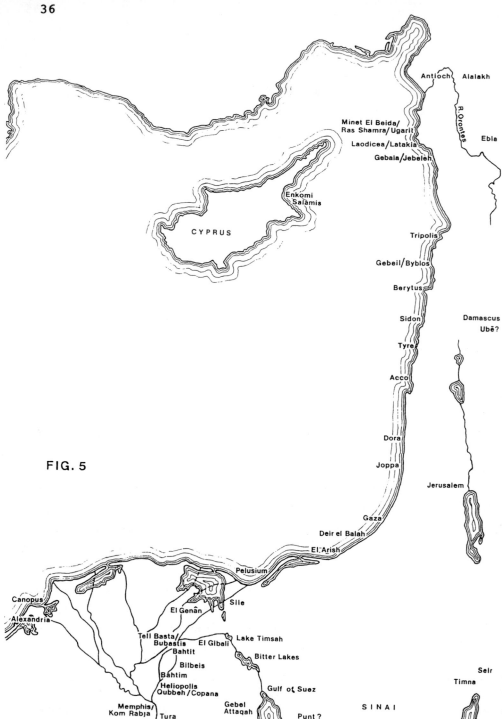

FIG. 5

Lake Mareotis which extends westwards along the coast, in the swampland near Taenia.[86] There was a tradition, current even in late antiquity, that the process of paper-making from the papyrus plant was "invented" at Memphis.[87] A paper-making industry is also recorded at Tanis in 256 B.C.[88] These places are included in our sketch map fig. 13.

It was emphasized by Lewis that papyrus had to be cut into strips and pressed together soon after it was picked, while the stems were still firm and upright and the starches in them still active to serve as a gluing agent. If this was indeed the method used in ancient times, it is not unreasonable to suppose that the place of manufacture was close to the place of the plant's growth. However, that is not the way that papyrus is manufactured now at The Institute of Papyrus on the Nile in Cairo by Dr. Ragab and his team. Here they have shown the importance of soaking the papyrus strips for 3-5 days in the same water, without changing it, before pressing them together. A recent Japanese experiment was reported by Shinabu Osawa on the significance of the "turbidus liquor" referred to by Pliny in the Bulletin of Kobe Women's College, no. 7 (1978), 63-8. There they found that after soaking the papyrus for a number of days, the paper becomes sticky and its odour putrescent. A microbiological examination revealed the presence of lactose-fermenting bacilli belonging to the Coli-aerogenes group. Today scientists are tending to believe that it is these bacilli which act as the gluing agent in papyrus, rather than the fresh sap of the stem.

The Egyptian delta is known to have been swampy in ancient times, particularly in its northern regions (see sketch map fig. 1). It therefore had the right conditions to produce papyrus, which is abundantly attested from ancient Egyptian sources as well as from classical writers. Strabo[89] tells us that in his day

papyrus did not grow as abundantly in the region of
Alexandria as it did in other parts of the delta. He
complained that the inhabitants of the delta did not
allow papyrus to grow everywhere in order to raise its
price. But it is very likely that the papyrus gradually
disappeared without much planning on the part of the
delta inhabitants, as the area was drained and farmed.
This would have destroyed the swampland which is vital
for its existence.

iv)   Which Gebal?

In her analysis of the problems concerning the name
of Byblos Emilia Masson drew attention to several
biblical variations on the Semitic root gbl-,[90] as in
Ezechiel 27,9, Joshua 13,5 and in St. Jerome's
Onomastica. The question must be asked whether these
variants all refer to the same geographical site. Some
doubt is cast on this, for example, by even a cursory
glance at the number of place-names derived from this
root, which are listed in the account of The Jewish War
by Josephus. There we find Gabaon (Biblical Gibeon),
Gabaa, Gabalis/Gobolis, Gabalites/Gobolites, Gebala,
Gebelos/Gibalu (Hebel), all of them being indisputably
different places, though firmly to be situated in
biblical lands and therefore not far from each other.

Even in the Amarna Letters[91] there are
differences in the rendering of Gubla, some of which are
clearly not dependent on the possible variations of the
vocalization of the cuneiform. For example, Amarna
Letter 74, which refers in lines 3 and 4 to Gubla,
written in the generally accepted way, has ^{alu}gub in
line 22. In Amarna Letter 139, line 33 refers to Gubla
written in the usual way, while lines 3, 8, 9 and 21
refer to ^{alu}gula which has been accepted as another

variant of <u>Gubla</u>, within the same letter. We also find
the form gub^{ub}li in Letters 129 and 362.

Knudtzon lists for us in his <u>Glossary</u> the various
ways in which <u>Gubla</u> is written in the Amarna Letters
68-140. We find:
alu$_{gub}$ki, alu$_{gu-ub-la}$, alu$_{gub-la}$,

alu$_{gub-la}$ki, alu$_{gu-ub-li}$ki, alu$_{ku-ub-li}$ki,

alu$_{gub-li}$, alu$_{gub}$ub-la, gu-la^{ki}, alu$_{gu-la}$,

alu ki$_{gub-la}$ (li), alani gub^{ub}-li-(la).

So far, no scholar has asked whether all these
variations, in close proximity to each other, can really
be referring to the same place. This problem could
usefully be discussed by the specialists in this field.
It is relevant to remind ourselves in this context that
in the seventy-two Amarna letters that we have relating
to <u>Gubla</u> (sic) their ruler is revealed to be only one man
for most of this period, namely Rib-Addi. Two of the
letters refer to one other man, Ilirabiḥ. It is
significant that neither of these two important people
are known from any monument in Gebeil/Byblos itself.
Furthermore we must remember that the provenance of these
letters is Egypt, not Gebeil/Byblos, or anywhere else in
the Near East.

From the second half of the twelfth century A.D. we
have the account of the wanderings of Benjamin of Tudela
who speaks of two cities of this similar name which lay
fairly close to each other along the Near Eastern coast.
The first one he mentions is "<u>Gebal</u> <u>(Gebala)</u>, which is
<u>Baal-Gad,</u> at the foot of the Lebanon".[92] It was
situated at two days' walk from <u>Lega</u> or <u>Ladikiya.</u>

The other city of the same name lay at one day's
journey from <u>Tripolis</u> or <u>Tarabulus El Sham.</u> He tells us:

"the other Gebal (Gubail) ... borders on the land

> of the children of Ammon ... the place is
> under the rule of the Genoese, the name of
> the governor being Guillelmus Embriacus.
> Here was found a temple belonging to the
> children of Ammon in olden times and an idol
> of theirs seated upon a throne or chair and
> made of stone overlaid with gold. Two women
> are represented sitting one on the right and
> one on the left of it, and there is an altar
> in front before which the Ammonites used to
> sacrifice and burn incense ... The place is
> situated on the sea-border of the land of
> Israel ... from there it is two days' journey
> to Beirut ..."[93]

René Dussaud[94] has compared the description of this second Gebal and its ancient shrine with the impressive discovery at Gebeil/Byblos in more recent times by Pierre Montet of a group of seated figures with a flat platform in front of them which could have served as an altar. These can be said to correspond with the description we have quoted from Benjamin of Tudela. It is therefore clear that the town excavated by Maurice Dunand[95] (and earlier by Pierre Montet and Ernest Renan) is the second one described by Benjamin of Tudela, the one we call Gebeil/Byblos today (see sketch map fig. 5).

The proximity of these two towns of the same name along that coast has probably given rise to confusion in the past. It is quite remarkable that the Karl Baedeker Guide to Syria and the Lebanon (1906, 334) describes Gebeil/Byblos, the town that we have hitherto accepted as being the biblical Gubal, as "an unimportant little town of 1000 inhabitants throughout which are scattered numerous fragments of ancient columns." Remarkably also, neither the earlier 1898 edition of his guidebook nor the later one refers to any kind of a harbour for this particular town, though its policy is to include this

aspect in its description of all the coastal cities and
towns. However, the guidebook dutifully quotes the
biblical references to the ancient Gubal, following the
traditional assumptions of the historians.

The town first described by Benjamin of Tudela is
called Jebeleh on page 412 of this same Baedeker
Guidebook. It is described as a poor village with 3000
inhabitants and as the capital of a district of that
name. We are told that its ancient name was Gebala. It
used to be a fortified city, situated at a small distance
from the sea, which had endured sieges in the past and
was situated in a fertile plain. Moreover, a harbour was
noted for this town by Baedeker. Like the other place of
the same name, this town had many antiquities lying about
in ruins. But remarkably, the Guide refers especially to
the numerous large hewn stones, some of which were eleven
feet in length and were used to protect the small
harbour. One of the characteristics of the biblical town
of this name was that its inhabitants were "hewers of
stone". This description fits the northern Gebala better
than Gebeil.

We must note that Strabo's description of
Byblos,[96] the first that we have from Greek sources,
tells us that it was situated "a short distance from the
sea". This could apply to the more northern town but not
to Gebeil/Byblos. Strabo also tells us that this city
lay in the plain which began at Laodiceia near Libanus,
which agrees with what Benjamin of Tudela said later for
the more northern town. Moreover, apart from the large
hewn stones that were noted by Baedeker for the northern
Jebeleh, and the harbour itself, we must emphasize that
it was situated at the foot of the Lebanon, where timber
for ship-building was presumably available and easily
accessible. This cannot be said for Gebeil/Byblos.
Historians have always had great difficulty in explaining
the associations of this town with ship-building

activity, as reported by Diodorus IX, 19:58 and others.

We must therefore acknowledge some serious doubts about the identity of the ancient Byblos as the biblical or the classical city. There is no natural harbour at Gebeil/Byblos. A recent description tells us: "The port, which is much silted up, lies west of the village. It consists of a cove formed by two great flat reefs and two jetties with towers at the end of them. It can only shelter small craft."[97] The reefs are shown on our sketch map fig. 6, based on Renan's first description of this coastline. The traveller Richard Pococke in 1745[98] omitted any reference to a port for "Esbele" Byblos, our Gebeil/Byblos, whereas he mentioned an important harbour for the more northern city which he calls Jebilee and which is referred to also in the literature as Gebala, Gabala and Jebeleh. Pococke also noted an amphitheatre remaining from classical times, which suggests some considerable status for the northern city.

Nassiri Khosrau described Djibal as the capital of a province of the same name which was situated in a central and important position and through which some ancient routes passed.[99] He is likely here to have had in mind Gebala/Jebeleh rather than Gebeil/Byblos because the archaeological evidence from this site does not point to active and continuous contact with the world at large for very long periods. On the other hand, the city of Gebala/Jebeleh was situated not only along a number of important ancient trade routes, but also in the middle of a well-watered and fertile plain, as well as being not far from the sea.

It is interesting to note in passing that the Amarna Letters 129 and 362 refer several times to the cities of Gubla, thus confirming that this city had some satellite towns, according to the pattern described by

Giorgio Buccellati in _Cities and Nations of Ancient Syria_ (1967), 40f. This could have applied to _Gebala_ rather than _Gebeil_.

But unfortunately we have practically no archaeological information for the northern Gebala. We are therefore ignorant as to the details of its early existence as a town, or as to its origins. We also cannot yet know of any possible early contacts with Egypt.

In her report on the pottery of the Gebala/Jebeleh region, Ann Ehrich recorded the receipt of an ivory seal at Qal'at er Rus, with the assurance that it had been found on that tell.[100] At that time Professor Albright happened to be present and he read the scarab "ḥ3tj-ᶜ n kpn Intin", namely, "the ruler of the land of Byblos, Intin". However, it is a fact, as Ehrich tells us in the report, that the man who had brought the scarab had proved unreliable in other circumstances so that it is not impossible that his statement concerning the place where the scarab was found might be inaccurate. Professor Albright himself appears to have been untroubled about the authenticity of the seal or the place where it was found. He also gave a secure date for it although no record is available of the place or level where it was found.[101] He suggested that it had come from "an Eighteenth Century grave some 150 km north of Byblos", thus illustrating, as he said, the scope of Intin's activity. But this particular seal, like most of those carrying the name of kpny, does not have an authenticated provenance. Very few of the scarab seals carrying this name and generally stated to have come from Gebeil/Byblos can be shown actually to have come from that site.

I am not disputing that this name was applied to Gebeil/Byblos in ancient times. This may well have been the case. But if <u>kbn/kpny</u> was the exact Egyptian equivalent of the Semitic <u>gbl</u>, the same name must have been used for a number of different places.

v) The "Gebal in Egypt" of the Phoenician Text.

One of the blocks said to have been found in Gebeil/Byblos, namely the remains of what was possibly a statue with the cartouches of Sheshonq I of the 22nd. dynasty, carries a text in Phoenician letters referring to "Abibaᶜal, king of Gebal ... and Gebal in Egypt" (see our fig. 7a here).[102]

We do not know even approximately where this block was found. It was bought early this century in Gebeil/Byblos by a diplomat called Loeytved, consul for Denmark in Beirut at that time.[103] The block is described as being of grey Egyptian granite, "certainly cut in Egypt".[104] If so, this would mean that the Phoenician inscription was also cut in Egypt. However, the fact that these Phoenician letters are incised around the cartouches suggests an afterthought or a postscript, possibly after the block arrived at a northern location, because no-one can argue that this Phoenician inscription is given a position on the block equal with that of the Egyptian cartouches.

Its earliest publication was by Ch. Clermont-Ganneau in 1903 as the result of a lecture on it to the French Academy,[105] with good photographs of a squeeze and of the block itself, and later again in 1905.[106] His translation of the Phoenician inscription was: "Qu'a érigé Abibaᶜal ... de Gebal, en Egypte, pour Baal-X ... citoyen de Gebal".[107]

Much attention has been given to this block over the years by a number of scholars. The translation of most of them, including Albright [108] and Montet,[109] agrees substantially with that offered by Donner and Röllig[110] and more recently by Gibson,[111] both accompanied by a good bibliography:

"[Votivbild, das herauf]brachte ꭓbb ͨl, König [von Byblos, Sohn des   Königs von] Byblos, von Ägypten (her) für die "Herrin von Byblos", seine Gebieterin ..."[112]

However, René Dussaud in Syria V (1924), 146 and in Syria VI (1925), 111 presented a different translation which should not be ignored. It agrees with Ch. Clermont-Ganneau inasmuch as he read in his text a Gebal in Egypt:

"Ont offert] Abiba ͨal, roi de Ge[bal et le Noge]sh de Gebal en Egypte à Ba ͨala[t-Gebal et à Ba] ͨal-Gebal ...".

As I myself am unfortunately unable to handle these texts which are nevertheless relevant to our general discussion here, I asked Dr. Sebastian Brock to explain to me the reason for such diverging translations. He very kindly and patiently offered me this explanation for which I am very grateful and which I shall pass on to those as inadequate as myself in this matter:

"The text clearly reads bmṣrm and b normally means in. But it so happens that in Ugaritic it can also mean from. On this basis it has been argued that b can also have this sense in both Phoenician and Hebrew. The interpretation of bmṣrm here is tied up with the restoration of the verb: Dussaud supplied a verb with the sense of donated, while Albright and others supplied a verb meaning brought, which of course requires to be

46

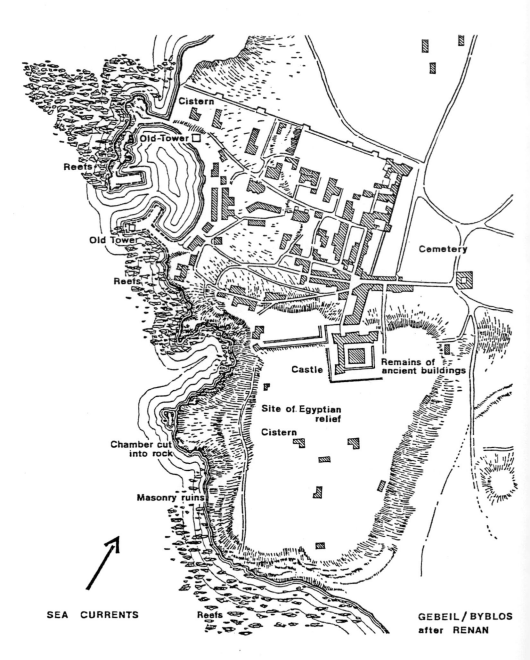

Cistern

Old Tower

Reefs

Old Tower

Reefs

Castle

Remains of
ancient buildings

Site of Egyptian
relief

Cistern

Chamber cut
into rock

Masonry ruins

Cemetery

SEA CURRENTS

Reefs

GEBEIL / BYBLOS
after RENAN

FIG. 6

followed by _from._ Unfortunately, only the
tail of the letter before the _aleph_ is left
and Albright categorically states, on the
basis of the hand copy in _Revue Biblique_
(1926), Plate VI, that this letter can only be
a _beth._ But an examination of the photograph
in Clermont-Ganneau, _Recueil d'arch. orientale_
VI, plate II and p. 74 makes it clear that the
tail of the letter in question is at the wrong
angle to be a _beth._ Thus the restoration
brought - the main basis for taking _b-_ in the
sense _from,_ rather than _in_ - is clearly
unacceptable."

It is therefore very likely that this inscription
is referring simultaneously to a _Gebal_ in the north and a
Gebal in Egypt. There is some hint here of the
"twinning" of these two towns of the same name. But
there are no clues as to where in Egypt this particular
Gebal might be. Indeed, if we did not have the
references to Baᶜalat and Baᶜal in conjunction with the
name of _Gebal_ in this inscription, we might reasonably
wonder whether this name does in fact refer to
Gebeil/Byblos, because Abibaᶜal is not known from any
other monument. We must emphasize again that there is no
proof that this block was actually found in
Gebeil/Byblos, only a seller's verbal assurance.

Before leaving this inscription we should draw
attention to another interpretation which we find in an
article by J. G. Février[113] who quotes O.
Eissfeldt.[114] Here bmṣrm is interpreted as having
nothing to do with Egypt but translated into German as
"in Not" or in French as "dans le cas de détresse".
However, unfortunately, Février also tells us that Abibaᶜal was King of Byblos in 925 and certainly the son of a
King of Byblos, without producing any evidence to this
effect.

The reconstruction of this block poses some problems. Because of a slight curve upwards at the top of the block which could correspond to the bottom of a seated figure wearing a pleated garment, it has been reconstructed as the bottom of a chair or a throne.[115] However, this is not where we would normally expect to find a king's cartouche, because the space under the throne was usually reserved for the portrayal of foreign enemies in an abject position. Alternatively we might expect to find there the union sign, representing, as we understand it at present, the union of Upper and Lower Egypt.[116]

We shall be returning to a discussion of the Gebal in Egypt in Part II, where we shall look at several aspects of this problem in separate sections, relating to the Egyptian material.

vi)   Some Relevant Archaeological Facts Concerning Gebeil/Byblos.

It is unfortunately the case that a very large proportion of the objects said to have come from Gebeil/Byblos, including much of the Egyptian material, did not come from a stratified and authenticated site but was merely bought there and elsewhere from dealers. Before we can make any sense of the Egyptian material said to have come from Byblos we shall need a detailed study of the provenance and context of each object. At present each Egyptian piece is listed with its appropriate bibliography in the Porter and Moss Topographical Bibliography, Vol. VI, pp. 386-392. Further bibliography is constantly being collected by them and is generously available to us all.

In order for a valid assessment to be made of these Egyptian objects as a whole, they should be studied by an archaeologist familiar with the Near Eastern material in order to ascertain the context in which they came to light, if this is at all possible. Such a study would also eventually reveal to us whether these Egyptian objects are likely to have been gifts, as appears to have been the case in the Royal Tombs of Gebeil/Byblos, or the result of trade in the case of objects of a lesser degree of perfection and of more practical use. We would not dispute the frequent occurrence of both these activities. We would dispute only that this city was a unique focal point in Egypt's horizon.

Above all, we must be careful about assigning any object to Gebeil/Byblos, Egyptian or otherwise, if it was not actually found there.

We have the example of the statue of Osorkon I, now in the Louvre, found by Wiedemann in Naples in 1881 in the possession of the banker Meuricoffre. Wiedemann described it in 1884 in his Ägyptische Geschichte[117] as two fragments of a large stone statue representing Osorkon I as a human-headed sphinx (sic). The other he thought to have been a piece of the base revealing a foot.[118] Photographs of both blocks were published in Dussaud's subsequent study in Syria VI (1925), Plate XXV and p. 102. These show clearly that the foot belongs to a standing figure and could not have been part of a sphinx. In 1895 Wiedemann published only the hieroglyphic inscription on the blocks,[119] without mentioning any other signs on them.

In 1912, it emerged[120] that the blocks had been in the possession of an antiquarian called Canessa before they were sold in Paris in 1910. It is not known how he acquired them. Only then was it stated that an alphabetic inscription was engraved on the bust of the statue. The sale catalogue mentions that "a Carian inscription" had been added subsequently. Dussaud translated this Phoenician inscription:

"Cette statue a fait Eliba⊂al, roi de Gebal,
en consé [cration à Ba] ⊂alat-Gebal par
lui-meme.   Qu'elle prolonge [les jours
d'E]liba⊂al et ses années (de règne) sur
[Gebal."[121]

René Dussaud argued strongly that this was not a forgery
because of the presence of an archaic kaph[122] which was
not recognized by the early scholars until the later
discovery of the tomb of Ahiram. However, conscious of
the fact that some material proof of the provenance of
this block would be welcome, Dussaud asked Virolleaud, at
that time in charge of the Antiquities Service in Syria,
to send two fragments in pink sandstone (grès rougeâtre)
which had been found by Montet at Gebeil/Byblos, to see
whether these could have been a part of this statue.[123]
When eventually these pieces arrived in the Louvre,
Barthoux found both Montet's fragment and the new Louvre
acquisition to be made of grès rose lustré from Mokattam,
near Cairo, but from different blocks, because Montet's
piece was lighter in colour than the statue. Thus no
archaeological proof exists of the provenance of this
block from Gebeil/Byblos. The evidence that we have
tells us that the stone and presumably the hieroglyphs
too were cut in Egypt (see fig. 7b).

It is an unfortunate fact that some distinguished
scholars have enjoyed transferring ancient inscriptions
from less valuable objects to more valuable ones or
vice-versa, as the occasion demanded. It is not
impossible that the Phoenician inscription may be a
genuine one, but transferred at a much later date to the
statue. We shall never know.

When Muntaha Saghieh wrote her thesis on Byblos in
the Third Millennium, which was published in 1983, she
set out to do something extremely difficult, namely to
reconstruct the stratigraphy and architecture of the
third millennium levels of this most disturbed site. Its

excavators, Renan, Montet and Dunand, had all complained of the disturbed state of the ground and none of them had attempted to present a rational and total picture of the material they found. This was the task that Muntaha Saghieh set herself and with meticulous care she established a level sequence for the archaeological material already published (see her Chapter One).

In doing this, inevitably, some new proposals were arrived at regarding the dates and cultural links of the various strata. It is interesting to note that in spite of the Phoenician inscriptions on some of the objects from Gebeil/Byblos, there is no evidence of a Phoenician city as such, for which the foremost requirement was a port.

Most important is Saghieh's description of the port of Byblos as a "modest creek which is 120 m long by 60 m wide."[124] The débris from past excavations has now covered most of the cliff so that it is impossible to establish a relationship between the city and the port such as it was or could ever have been.

An important characteristic of this city which is worth noting is that during its early life it had no walls.

The ceramic evidence for the beginning of Saghieh's period Byblos KI was found to be securely tied to the reign of King Djet/Den of the first Egyptian dynasty, and to the latter part of the Early Bronze I phase of Palestine.[125] However, while the names of all the kings of the dynasties IV-VI were found on alabaster vessels in the precincts of the Bala^cat temple or in the big audience hall, no inscription of any Egyptian king between Pepi II (Phiops II) and Sesostris I has been found at Byblos.[126] Furthermore, contrary to what had been claimed by distinguished scholars, Saghieh was able to

find no evidence of any direct link between Egypt and
Byblos in pre-dynastic times.[127]   Such evidence as had
been quoted by scholars was much more likely to belong to
the first Intermediate Period, she found.[128]   The pre-KI
Byblite ceramics (corresponding to pre-dynastic Egypt)
have a close affinity with Palestine, she found, but none
at all with Egypt.

Saghieh found that pottery similar to that of
period KI at Byblos was present in First Dynasty contexts
at Abydos, Saqqara, Lahun, Tarkhan and Helwan.[129]   But
the lack of contemporary Egyptian finds at Byblos as well
as the absence from Byblos of several of the major types of
foreign pottery found in Egypt indicates that there was
no direct trade at that time. Not only was this foreign
ware not to be found in Egypt before it was revealed in
the tomb of King Djer. But even then only one vessel
among the foreign wares has a close parallel with Byblos.
The others are consistent with the Palestinian EBI
ceramic styles. A similar pattern is found in the wares
from the tomb of Den at Saqqara and Djet in Tarkhan as
well as among the tomb vessels from Lahun.

This study carefully notes the objects which link
Egypt and Byblos as well as those which do not. One feels
that Saghieh dutifully seeks out all that can possibly
link Byblos with Egypt and she quotes the presence of
cedar in a Third Dynasty wooden coffin from the pyramid of
Djoser as indicating trade between Egypt and Byblos. But
as we have said in our opening remarks, this is most
unlikely on both geographical and practical grounds.
Cedar pollen has been found abundantly in the highlands of
the Sahara[130] and the Instruction for Merikare speaks
of mrw-wood as coming from the west.[131]   The
transportation of whole logs on those small ships
in ancient times from the Lebanon (sic) to Egypt was
impossible.

Among the early links with Egypt, Saghieh draws attention to the Baʿalat-Gebal temple of Byblos period KIV which appears to have been rebuilt along lines similar to King Sahurēᶜ's valley temple.[132]   The appearance of two alabaster fragments inscribed with the names of Neuserrēᶜ and Unas within this context seems to affirm this chronology.   She also quotes from the reliefs of Sahurēᶜ the fragments depicting an Asiatic bear and a Canaanite jug which is very similar to types A 8 and A 10 of Period KIV.

Saghieh's study of Byblite pottery shows the cultural development to be similar to Palestine in the EB, but she also notices some differences, by comparing the pottery with individual cities in Palestine.[133] Her chart, Table 9 (p.109), summarizes the results of her comparative studies of the pottery of this period, for Egypt, Byblos and Palestine.

The end of Saghieh's period KIV contains signs of destruction of the temples and major buildings.   Her following period JI reveals new architectural concepts as well as new ceramic styles.   This period seems to coincide with the end of the reign of Pepi II (i.e. approximately 2200 B.C.).   It has been suggested that this change was a dramatic one with the sudden intrusion of new ideas and a breaking away from the influence of Egypt.[134]

These new ideas have strong associations with the Syro-Anatolian cultural spheres.   The pottery of Byblos JI and JII links the city firmly with the northern countries and suggests for Saghieh the ethnic label "Amorite".

This state of affairs in Byblos at the end of the Third Millennium seems to be confirmed by Ora Negbi's study of the contacts between Byblos and Cyprus at this

period.[135]   This study of the contents of the deposit
within the "enceinte sacrée" showed that during the time
corresponding to the Egyptian First Intermediate Period
close relations were established between Byblos and other
sites in western Asia and Cyprus, with the abandonment of
strong links with Egypt.

The relations between Egypt and Gebeil/Byblos will
become much more difficult to assess in future if
Egyptologists eventually agree that the evidence points
to the fact that the name of kbn/kpny, as it is used in
the Egyptian texts, does not necessarily or exclusively
refer to that particular northern city. It means that in
considering this relationship, we must leave out of
account altogether the Egyptian references to the place
called kbn/kpny, including the important ones in the
Middle Kingdom story of Sinuhe.

However, to judge from the inscriptions found in
Gebeil/Byblos itself, contact with Egypt was clearly
resumed during the Twelfth Dynasty, and there is evidence
of contacts even during the New Kingdom period,
remarkably, because most of the site of Gebeil/Byblos
seems to have Roman levels over Middle Bronze levels, with
nothing in between.

Among the Middle Kingdom material from
Gebeil/Byblos we find:

- a small limestone fragment with the figure of
Isis seated on a low-back chair and the cartouche of
Sesostris I;[136]

- a bone cylinder inscribed with the name of
Ammenemes II;[137]

- a white round bead with the cartouche of Ammenemes
III which had been used as an amulet;[138]

        - an obsidian vase inscribed with the name of
Ammenemes III;[139]

        - an obsidian box with the name of Ammenemes IV
inscribed on the lid;[140]

        - another inscription of the name of Ammenemes IV
was found on the lid of a grey stone vase.[141]

        There is other material which has been accepted as
Egyptian but which is insecure as to its original
archaeological context or original inscription, now
damaged and unreadable. A few objects found in the Royal
Tombs, which date to the Middle Kingdom, are recognizably
Egyptian though not inscribed, such as the silver mirror
with gold ornamentation on the handle and the gold
pendant and gold pectoral,[142] both from Tomb II.
Others from the Royal Tombs and elsewhere are not so
certainly to be accepted as Egyptian, though perhaps
Egyptianizing, in style.

        The Temple of the Obelisks excavated by Dunand[143]
appears to correspond in date to the Middle Kingdom. It
was moved to allow further excavation of this site.
However, it is important to remember that many of the
obelisks found there had already been re-used at that
stage of the site's history, one obelisk appearing to
cover a foundation deposit,[144] others being
incorporated into the walls and the paving of this site.
This means that the Temple of the Obelisks had flourished
in a period earlier than the Middle Kingdom. This name,
given to it by Dunand was more impressive than the site
itself, observed Montet.[145] Although over thirty
obelisks had been found in this area by the excavator,
only the middle one of a standing group of three had any
inscriptions on it. Remarkably enough, the two lines of
writing on this obelisk were in Egyptian hieroglyphs and
were placed not on the front of the obelisk, as one might

expect, but on its eastern side as it stood. The hieroglyphs were published by Montet[146] (from whose reading we have adapted our fig. 14 here) and he translated them:

"L'aimé d'Hérichef-Rē, le prince de Byblos Abichemou, renouvelé de vie, son scelleur royal, Koukou, fils de Routaouy (ou de Routata) juste de voix."[147]

Remarkably, a number of fragments datable to the New Kingdom were found on this site, a number of them bearing the name of Ramesses II. This fact is remarkable because at Gebeil/Byblos the Middle Bronze Period, corresponding roughly to the Middle Kingdom of Egypt, was situated immediately under the Roman levels over most of the site. The excavators found no evidence of an Iron Age or any other intermediate period. It must be remembered however, that even before Renan had begun excavations here the area had been severely disturbed and the stratifications destroyed.

A fragment now in the Beirut Museum carries the cartouche of Ramesses II. This piece is believed to have been part of a monumental doorway.[148] Three large stelae of Ramesses II carved on the mountain side at Nahr El Kelb[149] have been explained by scholars as evidence that the pharaoh had visited this area. This may or may not have been the case. Montet found fragments of Egyptian scenes, one of which carried the name and titles of Ramesses II.[150] In Ahiram's tomb shaft a piece of alabaster carried the name of Ramesses II while another in the tomb itself bore his cartouche.[151] This has led scholars to believe that Ahiram and Ramesses II were contemporaries.

Dunand was struck by the number of pieces bearing the name of Ramesses II.[152] No other Egyptian monarch of the New Kingdom appears to have been so well-known at Gebeil/Byblos, however.

All that we can safely say about the Egyptian material found at Gebeil/Byblos is that it indicates close contacts at some stages in the history of that city. However, with the greater number of sites now being excavated in the Near East, this city has now ceased to be the only one which could produce Egyptian material at some distance from Egypt. We must now try to see this city from a more realistic perspective. As we hope to show in the following pages, the Gebal in Egypt is a very complex problem indeed and if we look at that in stages, we shall see how the city of Gebeil/Byblos recedes into a much less important background of Egypt than we have accepted during the last hundred years.

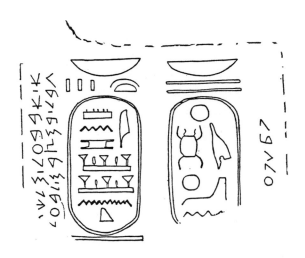

FIG. 7**a**   after   Montet

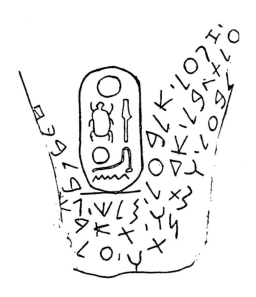

FIG. 7**b**   after   Montet

PART TWO

SOME FRESH PROPOSALS FOR FACING THIS PROBLEM

vii) The kbn/kpny of the Egyptian texts.

It is eminently indicative of the state of our
science that the entry under Byblos in the comparatively
recent Lexikon der Ägyptologie, written by its editor,
Wolfgang Helck, does not even remotely concern itself
with any reasons as to why kbn/kpny should be accepted as
Gebeil/Byblos. This assumption is taken for granted and
upon this unjustified acceptance a great case is built on
the relations between Egypt and the Near East. Not only
does this author not concern himself with the early
discussion of this name among the Egyptologists and
others. He also persists in saying, against the total
absence of evidence to this effect, that the Egyptians
went to sea in ships bearing this name.[153]

We have already pointed out the difficulties which
were recognized by Max Müller and Raymond Weill in
equating the Egyptian names of kbn/kpny with the
particular town of Gebeil/Byblos. Some doubts on this
equivalence for the near Eastern area were also expressed
by E. Eisler[154] and P. Mallon.[155] The lack of
evidence for linking Gebeil/Byblos to many ancient texts
also prompted Anneliese Kammenhuber to ask: "Ist Byblos
sicher?".[156] Rightly so.

As we said earlier, it was Chabas who established
the equivalence of kbn/kpny with the Semitic root gbl.
The finding at that time by Renan of some Egyptian
objects inscribed with hieroglyphs at Gebeil/Byblos
established a firm link between the two. But it was not
until Adolf Erman and Kurt Sethe published their articles
on this topic in 1900 and 1908 - both rather flimsy

efforts from these two outstanding scholars - that the myth of the equivalence of kbn/kpny with the particular town of Gebeil/Byblos became irrevocably established.[157] It is surprising that these two great scholars discussed this equivalence without any reference to the original analysis by Chabas in 1866. No scholar today would find the arguments they offered then at all convincing. But there followed further approval for this idea from Montet,[158] Dussaud[159] and above all, from Alan Gardiner.[160] It is therefore not surprising that no-one has seen fit to question these conclusions until now, when more information is available to us.

We must bear in mind the fact that this equation seemed right at that time because it was firmly believed that ꜥš meant cedar and that the ancient Egyptians had to go to the Lebanon to get it. Renan's early finds of Egyptian objects at Gebeil/Byblos simply confirmed this belief.

However, we now have two important reasons for re-assessing this idea. Firstly, ꜥš does not mean cedar, but probably pine.[161] There is now scientific evidence to show that there were rich oak and pine forests in southern Palestine from pharaonic times until our own.[162] The cedar that was used in ancient times may well have come from a region west of the Nile as we know that the Saharan regions of Hoggar and Tibesti have produced cedar pollens at levels which could coincide with the early dynastic period of Egypt.[163] Secondly, if the ancient Egyptians had excellent pine and other timber growing possibly as far south as the eastern delta, they had no need at all to go to Gebeil/Byblos to get any. The fact that Egyptian hieroglyphic inscriptions were found in that city is no longer as significant as it was at first, because there have now been other such finds from other sites such as Kition in Cyprus,[164] Ras Shamra,[165] Deir el Balah[166] and others. Thus Gebeil/Byblos is no longer unique in yielding such objects. An understanding of this background is essential in considering the identity of the Egyptian kbn/kpny.

There are not many examples of this name in the early dynastic period. They are found more frequently in the Middle Kingdom and they are again more numerous in later periods as Henri Gauthier[167] has shown.

The earliest example of this name occurs as kbn in the Old Kingdom tomb of Khui, in Aswan, published by J. De Morgan, Catalogue des Monuments, Vol. 1 (1893), 157 (see our fig. 8 here). However, Sethe altered this name to k3š when he transcribed this text into his Urkunden I, 140, last line on that page. Then, after consulting with Gardiner, Sethe reconsidered this and accepted kbn here, as meaning Gebeil/Byblos. He explains his position on this in his fundamental article on this topic in 1908,[168] to which we have already referred. This text tells us that Khui and his companion had returned safely from kbn and Punt. This suggests, rightly I believe, that the two sites lay in the same general direction, a point to which we shall be returning below. Nevertheless we can see why Sethe wanted to associate Punt with k3š rather than with kbn, because both those sites have, since the earliest readings of these texts, been associated with the south, wrongly I believe. I have discussed this elsewhere.[169] Although kbn and Punt are mentioned together in some texts, most scholars have assumed them to lie in totally opposite directions, without ever questioning the basis for these assumptions.

Another early reference to kbn is in the Old Kingdom inscription of Pepinakht, in which a kbnt vessel is referred to.[170] These boats are believed to have acquired this name because they were built for the kbn journey and it is worthy of note that it is these same

62

FIG. 8a   after   De Morgan

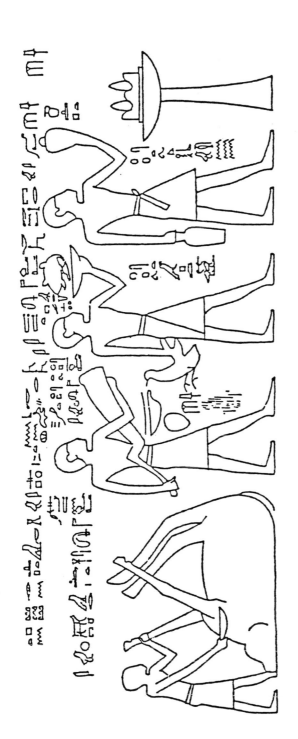

FIG. 8b   Detail

vessels that are sent to Punt, presumably because of
their size and storage space, which is another link
between these two places. Sethe's early discussion[171]
shows these transport vessels to have been written both
as kbnwt and kpnwt from the Middle Kingdom onwards, each
with the same determinative (see our fig. 10). We can
therefore be fairly certain that both of these writings
are used for the same kind of vessel. In the ninth
campaign of the Annals of Tuthmosis III,[172] this type
of boat is listed with Keftiu and Sekhtu vessels, both
names related to groups of people.

If it were not for the fact that the vessels called
kbnwt and kpnwt seem to be of the same type, we should be
prompted to ask whether we can be absolutely certain that
kbn and kpny are indeed referring to the same place at
all times. Paton[173] made the interesting point that in
five Pyramid Text examples, the kp sound is written with
the censer and the meaning is related to the use of
incense. It follows therefore that the ancient Egyptians
of that time could perfectly well convey the sound of
kpny had they wished. Yet the Old Kingdom form of this
place-name appears to be kbn and we have to accept that
the easing of the b to p in this name took place during
the Middle Kingdom, when both forms are to be found.

Apart from the fact that this place-name is written
with a p sound from the Middle Kindgom onwards, some
doubts are also raised by the number of variations in the
writing of kbn/kpny, as Gauthier had already noted. Our
fig. 11 shows that this name is very often written with
the Old Kingdom type of censer, but later in the New
Kingdom both the hand and the lion's claw are used to
convey the sound of kp, and it is often written without
the final consonant.

In the Middle Kingdom we find the Coffin Texts
following the earlier tradition of kbn (see our figs. 10,

11). However, during this same period we also find some variations in the writing of this name among the Sinuhe texts. Gardiner discussed the problem of the writing of this name in Sinuhe in his commentary.[174] It differs in the various versions of this story that have come down to us. Gardiner remarked that the hieratic sign for kp had been inverted and he quoted a similar writing in the Griffith Hieratic Papyri from Kahun and Gurob (Plate 28, III, 2 line 5). Clère[175] too discussed this point and found this inversion also in the execration texts published by both Sethe and Posener. However the significance of this is not clear.

Thus, while it seems that we must accept all these readings as kbn/kpny, the understanding of Gebeil/Byblos for this name in Sinuhe or anywhere else in no more than a tacit agreement by a major group of scholars. There is no proven certainty about it. The adherence of Von Bissing, Meyer and Sethe to this view no doubt lent weight to it and gratified Gardiner,[176] while the non-adherence of Maspéro and Weill irritated him, but did not deflect him from this view, which became the established one.

What is particularly disturbing is that all the arguments begin and end with the assumption that the hieroglyphic and hieratic writing of kbn/kpny can only be referring to Gebeil/Byblos and to no other place, because this is the only site which the Egyptologist has until now recognized as important enough to fit this context. This affects profoundly our understanding of many texts and consequently, some important aspects of the history of ancient Egypt.

It should be repeated here in passing that although we always assume the story of Sinuhe to be the story of an Egyptian, it is quite possible that it may be otherwise. I have already suggested elsewhere[177] that it is very likely from the details given in the story that he may have been a foreigner who was raised in Egypt in the highest kind of service, as many foreigners were, namely in the royal palace attending the family of the Pharaoh. His keen knowledge of the foreign areas along Egypt's borders is not consistent with that of an ordinary servant and many details in his story are much more acceptable and logical if we accept them as coming from one who had returned to a former background from which he had sprung.

There are huge and irrational gaps between the areas that Egyptologists are willing to consider to fit the many as yet unidentified place-names in the texts. Reason alone suggests that there must have been foreign towns of some importance along the borders of ancient Egypt and in areas not too far removed from them. Many of the foreign names on the long lists of enemy captives must have been situated in the eastern desert and in the Sinai. This is applicable also to our acceptance of kbn/kpny. In the absence of any proof that it lay overseas, we must consider the possibility that it may have been situated on inland water, yet in non-Egyptian territory.

My rejection of Gebeil/Byblos as the acceptance for kbn/kpny requires that some other place be proposed for it. This is a separate problem and a very complex one, as we shall see.

If we were to relate this ancient name to one that sounds like it today, which may have endured since ancient times and which may have represented a desirable stopping-place away from Egypt proper, we might suggest Canopus (or Canobus) or even Copana, both shown on our sketch map fig. 5.

The suggestion of Canopus or Canobus[178] which

lies on the coast near Abukir, approximately twenty kilometres east of Alexandria, should certainly gladden the heart of all those who adhere to the sea-going theory for the ancient Egyptians. Yet I cannot offer this as a serious suggestion because it does not fit the requirements that must be attached to an identification of kbn/kpny, above all that it must be a place from which timber was obtained. The Canopus canal lies too close to the present shoreline and to the banks of silt to have been an ancient site for a forest. We know too from the Renaissance travellers that in the natural state there were salt flats between Alexandria and Abukir.

We find the geographical name of Copana in the account of the traveller Jean Palerne Forésien in 1581.[179] It was the place where the caravans assembled to go to Suez. There his party, consisting of 800-odd camel-loads, collected water and provisions before setting out. Nearby there was a fine building supported by pillars and painted in the arabesque style which was used by the pachas at that time as a kind of arsenal. The exact position of this site is described as three or four miles north of Cairo, at Matariyah, in fact, just beyond Abbassiyah today. Some writers have called this site Qubbeh (written also Kubbeh) and it was reached by following the route of the present irrigation canal northwards. It is striking that the name of Qubbeh can be closely related to the word kȝp, incense (WB V, 103). Bearing in mind that Copana/Qubbeh was traditionally a place where caravans gathered in order to set out on a long journey into foreign territory, it might well be that this is where offerings of food and incense were made to the gods as is described in the story of Henu of the Eleventh Dynasty.[180] It is not impossible that Qubbeh may have derived its name from the fact that it was a place where incense was offered.[181] Similarly it must be accepted that incense and other offerings would be made also at the place of arrival, by way of giving

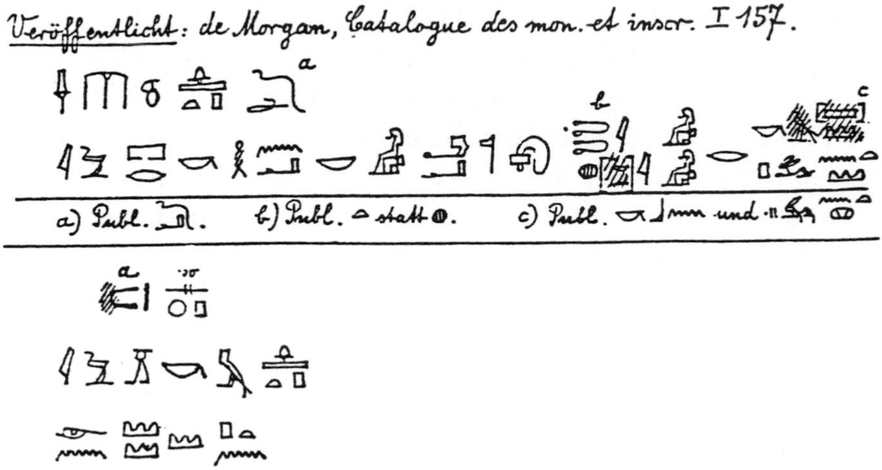

Veröffentlicht: de Morgan, Catalogue des mon. et inscr. I 157.

a) Publ. ⟨glyph⟩. b) Publ. ⟨glyph⟩ statt ⟨glyph⟩. c) Publ. ⟨glyph⟩ ⟨glyph⟩ und .II ⟨glyph⟩ ⟨glyph⟩

FIG. 9   Sethe,   Urk. I   140 f.

a   b

FIG. 10

thanks for a journey safely completed. We should not exclude the possibility that this name may have its roots in the activity of offering incense, and it may not be accidental that a garden of incense-trees (balsamum) was to be found at Matariyah nearby, as is recorded from mediaeval times onwards. I have discussed this elsewhere.[182]

On the physical level there are some substantial facts about kbn/kpny which we cannot overlook.

Firstly, it was the source of the $^c\check{s}$-wood which was used by the ancient Egyptians. We can now be certain that this term does not mean cedar so that there is no need to associate kbn/kpny with Gebeil/Byblos for this reason. The fact that this term is most likely to mean pine means that kbn/kpny should be sought between the eastern delta and southern Palestine, where we know that a flourishing forest of oak and pine existed from pre-biblical times until the First World War in our own era. If this does not seem far enough away from Egypt to satisfy some scholars, it is because they have not traversed sufficiently long distances on foot or by donkey.[183]

Secondly, in kbn/kpny we have a name which is accompanied only by the hill-country determinative in the Egyptian texts. Not until the very late story of Wenamun do we have a town determinative accompanying the hill-country. It is probable therefore that this site did not become a town until relatively late times.

Thirdly, it is a place to which the same vessels went as those that were sent to Punt. In the Old Kingdom text of Khui[184] we are told that he and his companion Tty went to both kbn and Punt, as though it were in the same direction (our fig. 8). The text of Pepinakht of approximately the same period tells us that a kbnt vessel

was used to go to Punt.[185]   An Eleventh Dynasty text
from the Wadi Hammamat tells us that Henu was entrusted
with the task of dispatching a kbnjjt vessel to
Punt.[186]

I have already discussed the evidence for Punt in
some detail elsewhere[187] and have suggested that,
taking all of it into account, the only way it fits
together and makes sense is to place Punt in the central
western Sinai (see our fig. 13). This is supported by
the references in the Egyptian texts to bj3 and Punt
together. As we shall see below, it also makes much more
sense to fit kbn into this same general direction because
this is what the texts themselves suggest.[188]

Fourthly, according to a Middle Kingdom Coffin
text, jurisdiction over this place was in the hands of
the goddess Hathor, whose list of titles includes not only
lady of kbn but also lady of Punt. This Coffin Text from
Bersheh[189] tells us that Hathor, the lady of kbn, makes
the steering oars for the vessels of the dead. We know
that Hathor was closely related to the foreign borders of
Egypt, particularly with the pink mountains and the
papyrus marshes, both of which must be considered to have
lain outside the territory of ancient Egypt proper.
Moreover she is associated in the texts with favourable
winds[190] without which the ancient travellers on
dangerous foreign waters, albeit of the Nile, would be
unable to reach their destination. To be becalmed in
hostile waters, even along their own Great River or a
swollen wadi branching off from it, was a dangerous
predicament to be avoided at any cost. In such
circumstances, both lives and valuable cargo were put at
risk.

The earliest reference to Hathor to be found on
Egyptian fragments from Gebeil/Byblos is a cylinder seal
of the Fourth Dynasty in which Hathor is associated with

Chephren.[191]   Other fragments of Egyptian monuments
found at this site also bear her name.[192]   But it was
Adolf Erman who established the belief that Hathor was
the goddess of Gebeil/Byblos in his original article of
1905, to which we have already referred.   He argued that,
as that city had a female protector-god and as we find
Hathor referred to in the ancient Egyptian texts as nbt
kpny, it must be she who presided over that city.   This
title is found on the Coffin Texts, as we have already
said, in some women's names in various documents and on
the Turin statuette, all to be dated no earlier than the
Middle Kingdom.

The   Turin   statuette[193]   whose   provenance   is
unfortunately not known is illustrated here in our Plates
I and II.   It bears the Turin Museum catalogue number
3036 and inventory number 5544.   It is of white limestone
and 0.28 m high, broken at the foot.   Maspéro suggested
that the woman holding the Hathor column in front of her
represented a priestess.   The fact that her face and
hands are painted a dark red led some scholars to suggest
that this might be the representation of a man and not a
woman, but it may well be a realistic portrayal of a
woman belonging to an ethnic group of dark red skin.

The   inscription   itself   does   not   help   us   to
understand this figure.   The inscription on the column
refers to Hathor as the patroness of peace, of the foreign
country of kp(ny) and of the foreign country of w3w3jj.
The inscription on her back tells us that she is the lady
of the foreign land of the west and of the heavens as
well, as though to encompass the whole world.

It must be emphasized that Hathor is not known by
this name in any non-Egyptian text from Gebeil/Byblos or
any other Near Eastern site.   Among the growing volume of
material available to us today we never find her
represented anywhere in the Near East with the cow face

and ears that she has in the Egyptian iconography. This
absence of any textual reference to this name or any
pictorial representation of her on non-Egyptian documents
applies as much to Gebeil/Byblos as elsewhere. There is,
however, one example which might be described as an
attempt at adaptation of this goddess for local worship.
It is the upper part of the stela of Yehavmelek where we
see a seated goddess wearing on her head a disc between
two horns and holding a papyrus sceptre[194] (fig. 15).
But this is an exception which proves the rule. The
early cultures of the Near East and the Aegean have
yielded evidence for the worship of female gods and
Gebeil/Byblos is no exception in having Baᶜalat as well
as Baᶜal. At the same time it must be acknowledged that
the Egyptian goddess Hathor, who had such close
affinities with the foreign borders of Egypt, has
remained to a large extent an enigmatic concept, worthy
of much further study.

viii) My Identification of kbn/kpny as El Gibali

     Whether kbn/kpny is indeed firmly to be accepted as
the Egyptian equivalent of the Semitic gbl I cannot
myself confirm or deny. It seems that the linguists
consider this to be quite acceptable. So without the
pre-judgement that it has to be Gebeil/Byblos, we should
try to fit this suggestion to the requirements of this
site as is indicated in the Egyptian documents.

     If kbn/kpny is to be equated with the name of gbl
in an area which the palaeo-botanists tell us was rich in
timber in the not-so-distant past, which was reached by
water through hostile territory and which lay in the
easterly direction of Punt according to the textual
evidence, we are able to suggest a place that was some
fifty years ago an enormous mound south-west of Lake

Timsah, called El Gibali (see our sketch maps figs. 12 and 13). We must remember that Lake Timsah was a sweet water lake until the Suez Canal was cut and that hippopotamus remains were found in it. Furthermore this lake extended further into the surrounding swamps before the cutting of the canal, right through the centre of it. This served to some extent as a drainage feature in this area, which was supplemented in due course by the cultivation of the surrounding lands.

El Gibali was situated within the swampland surrounding this lake and it was probably not the only kom in this area isolated by water, probably continuously and not only as the result of a high inundation.

My thanks must be offered yet again to the Governor of Ismailia, Mr. Abdul Moneim Emara and his most efficient and helpful team in the Public Relations Department, Mr. Mahmoud Ibrahim, Miss Fatma Mansour and Mr. Mohammed Hassan Ibrahim, all of whom helped me to understand the geography of this region. The latter officer actually found the area formerly occupied by this mound called El Gibali, because today most of it has disappeared under the bull-dozers. Only a very small extension of this ancient mound of El Gibali is still standing today and it is called Gebal Mariam. There is a modern obelisk on top of it which the engineer/Egyptologist Georges Goyon helped to erect some years ago (see our Plates III-VI). The soil of this small remaining part of this mound is full of broken pottery which has never been studied. The soil of the encroaching cultivation on the area where the mound used to be (see Plate IV) is also full of sherds.

No archaeological or stratigraphical study of this mound has ever been made and it is now too late. In February 1982 when I was there last the bull-dozers were working clearing large areas of the mound. The claw

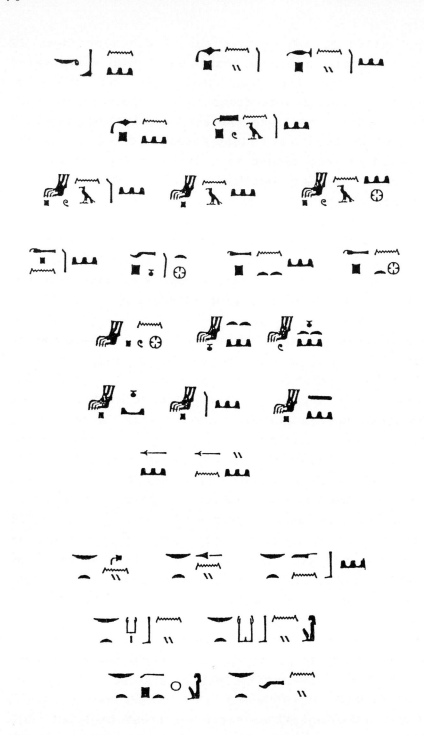

FIG. 11 – after Gauthier

marks of the bull-dozers are clearly to be seen on the photographs showing the side of the kom, on Plates III-VI.

I spoke to three elderly men in the district of El Gibali: Ali Said Hassan Refai Hussein El Hawy, Hussein Ali Salama and Barakat Mansour Id. They told me that in their youth El Gibali had been a kom stretching some six kilometres south-west of Lake Timsah from Gebal Mariam, as far as the present irrigation canal. This area is now flat, cultivated land, but teeming with broken pottery.

It is very important to note that this general area is still very swampy in places, even though it has in recent years been extensively drained for farming. Swampland is in fact shown in this area on the maps prepared by the Napoleonic Survey early in the nineteenth century and it was still there in the maps prepared by the Survey of Egypt some fifty years ago. Clearly in earlier times this was an area of thick swamps and it is likely that they enveloped a number of islands within them, thus cutting them off from the neighbouring lands, except by boat.

This is evident also from the name of the lake itself, Timsah, which is certainly derived from t3 msḥ, the land of the crocodile. We know that crocodiles need swampland in order to thrive. It is probably because of the gradually disappearing swampland that the crocodile died out in that region.

Furthermore, we know that the natural depression eastwards of the Wadi Tumilat took the Nile water to Lake Timsah during the inundation without impediment until artificial barriers were built to prevent this from happening.[195] We can be sure of this because during a particularly high Nile inundation in 1800 A.D., the artificial barriers were ruptured and the Nile water again reached Lake Timsah along this natural drainage channel, the Wadi Tumilat.[196] That is, after all, what a _wadi_ is. There is therefore no need for scholars to try to deny that any waterway existed there until very late in the pharaonic period.[197] The Napoleonic Survey's geographical map Plate 31 tells us, in indicating Lake Timsah, that there was no water in it except during the high inundations of the Nile. This must have been true at least during the time in which that survey was made.

If it was true even in earlier times that the water of the Nile would fill Lake Timsah only in times of high flooding, it would follow that journeys from Egypt to the Sinai and Punt by water could not have taken place in seasons of low water. Similarly, if _kbn/kpny_ is equated with _El Gibali_ that water route too would in this hypothesis only have been possible in high Nile seasons.

In this context it should be remembered that the Egyptian cargo vessels were large to allow for the carrying of substantial quantities of goods on their decks.[198] Such vessels would require a considerable depth of water, the more so when they were laden, which was probably the case both on their way out and on their way home. We should also bear in mind the fact that during a high inundation, the Nile water at the end of its journey in the delta was very fast and very dangerous because of the mounds and the silting up of the turtlebacks. We shall be discussing in detail the hazards of such travel in our forthcoming study of the journey of Wenamun, considered in the light of our fresh geographical proposals for _kbn/kpny_.

The acceptance of _kbn/kpny_ as _El Gibali_ would satisfy all the requirements of the texts. It is in an area that was well provided with water, hence fertile. It was a large mountain extending for a number of

77

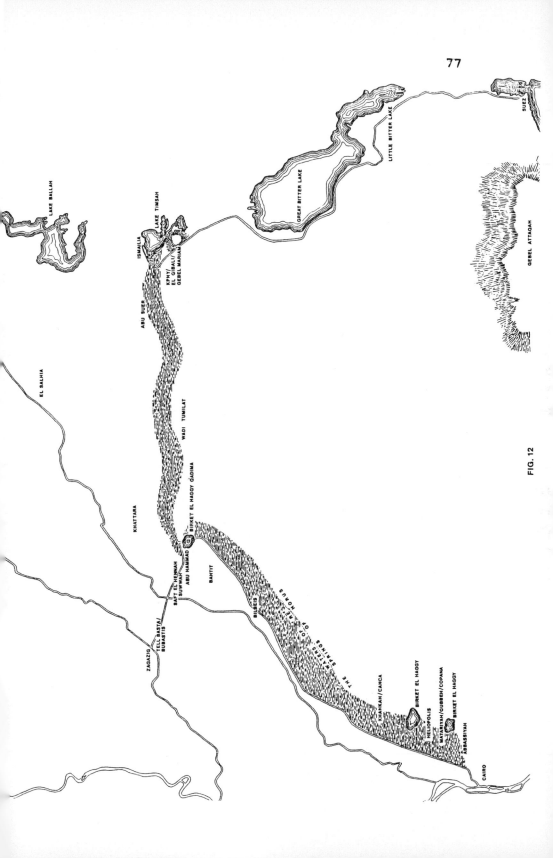

FIG. 12

kilometres and therefore not merely a town thus justifying the usual hill-country determinative, without the town sign. It is very possible that Hathor had a shrine or a cult there, just as she had in Timna[199] and in Serabit El Khadim in the Sinai.[200] Lastly, the journey to this site followed the same route as the one used to go to bj3, the Sinai, and Punt (see our figs. 12 and 13), all three being situated in the same general easterly direction away from Egypt, as we are told by the texts.[201]

It is perhaps a great deal to ask of scholars that they should exercise enough flexibility to apply logic to the totally unbased assumptions which prevail in the Egyptological textbooks today and which they were taught as truths by their seniors. Yet this will have to be done, sooner or later. It is wholly unacceptable that Egyptological reviewers and critics should ignore the evidence I have presented and simply reassert the traditional assumptions. That is neither scholarly nor scientific and it ought not to be acceptable to the editors of serious journals. Before any Egyptologist can be allowed to dismiss my arguments from the evidence as "theoretical", or even as "nonsense" as one distinguished scholar said,[202] he must produce what evidence he has to justify his adherence to the old assumptions.

Many of the historical concepts which fill our Egyptological textbooks today are, when we examine them closely, no more than opinions expressed by some of the great early scholars, whom we still quite rightly revere.

ix) An Ancient City in Egypt called Byblos and unrelated
     to kbn/kpny.

A passage from Ctesias in Photius[203] describes
the revolt of Inaros, a Libyan prince believed to be the
son of Psammeticus, against the Persian rule in Egypt
around 460 B.C. We are told that, with his Greek allies,
Inaros took refuge in a fortified town of Egypt called
Byblos, which proved to be impregnable and which he left
only after guarantees had been given by the enemy.
Scholars must treat Ctesias with a certain amount of
caution, because his work has come down to us through
other writers and in fragments. However, fortunately for
us, the sections from Photius telling us this story,
generally numbered as sections 32-35 in the scholarly
editions, are considered to be fairly accurate because it
has been possible to compare them with accounts of these
same events by Thucydides i, 104 ff. and Herodotus iii,
12 and vii, 7. Also Diodorus xi, 71 and 74-5. They have
all been found to agree substantially with each other in
the facts they present, although the place-names in their
accounts differ. Only Ctesias names a Byblos in Egypt.
The name Herodotus gives to his fortified town is
Papremis and we know that this is one of the very few
occurrences of this particular name that we have. It
would follow that when we have found the ancient Egyptian
Byblos we have also found Papremis. The problem is
complex and interesting and closely associated with
environmental factors, as we shall see.

It is fortunate for us that Stephen of Byzantium
also referred to a fortress town called Byblos in
Egypt[204] which, he tells us, was situated on the road
leading from Heliopolis to Bubastis (see our sketch map
fig. 13).

We must go back in time for a moment to emphasize

that any town of early date that was built in the Delta, before the establishment of a regular control of the annual inundation of the Nile,[205] would have been built on a natural or artificial height that would remain above the highest possible floodwater without being threatened by it each year. There is no likelihood that papyrus could have grown on such an elevation, because it would have been too well-drained. The only way in which papyrus could be associated with an elevated site would be for this town to have been situated in the middle of a swampland.

If we look for a fortified town on the road from Heliopolis to Bubastis, in the middle of an ancient swampland, with a name that can be related to Byblos, we are again fortunate. We have Bilbeis (see our sketch map fig. 13).

The traveller Menusham Ben R. Menahem, who in 1481 travelled along this road, spoke of a town called Bilibis.[206] In 1591, the Dutch traveller Jan Sommer[207] referred to a return journey to Cairo from the Red Sea, through a town called Bubelis, which the geographical context allows us to identify as the present-day Bilbeis. According to this writer, he and his group arrived at the town called Ramses before reaching Bubelis, a fact which agrees with the account of Stephen of Byzantium as well. We know that the Ramesside headquarters in the Delta was called "The House of Ramesses" but it has not yet been established where it was situated[208] exactly, though it was in this general area.

An earlier traveller in 1482-3, Joos van Ghistele,[209] referred to a town called Burbays in this same area. He called it a densely-populated city and said of it:

"One finds a well-cultivated and well-planted region, with plenty of pastureland for the animals until one finally arrives at a place called Burbays, which was formerly a very large and very solid town surrounded by thick walls in fired bricks. This town had several gates, the outline of which are still visible. It is well-built and thickly populated, having approximately the importance of Courtrai in Flanders. It is situated at a four days' journey from Catya. The Jews living there say that the region around the town and stretching as far as the Nile in the direction of Damietta used to be called the land of Gessen in the Old Testament."

It is clear from the reports of all the ancient travellers through this region that Bilbeis was a fortified town situated in the middle of a well-watered and fertile region. This fact is not obvious today as the desert has greatly encroached in this area. But it is clear that this city lay along the well-beaten route which the ancient pilgrims and merchants followed to go in and out of Egypt.[210]

Serge Sauneron[211] made the important point that most caravans had to stop outside a city in order to have the space to spread out their animals, their tents and their goods. Many early travellers refer to the tall trees offering shade outside the walls of Bilbeis and the excellent and abundant water to be found there.[212]

In the record of his journey in 1665-6, Antonius Gonzales tells us:[213]

"... We left Canca at four o'clock in the morning, along a completely flat road, with fields everywhere, very fertile because of the abundance of water. I saw innumerable wells, one at hardly a stone's throw from the other. There are two villages between Canca and Bilbeis, which are at a distance of two leagues from each other ... we erected our tents outside the town but quite close to it, on flat, even ground under some tall trees, believing that it was within its boundaries ... Half of the town, towards the north and east, was surrounded by a medium-sized shrub called henna ... On the other side of the town, some very special gardens were to be found and some palm plantations, almost forests."

These details are confirmed by other early travellers from Europe. Aquilante Rocchetta, who was there in 1599,[214] earlier than the writer we previously quoted, also referred to the abundant and excellent water of the many springs in that area. Travelling southwards from Khattara (see our fig. 13), Rocchetta noted both on his right and left water reservoirs resembling lakes in which were to be seen a great abundance of fish. However, none of the travellers of this period refer to papyrus in the vicinity of Bilbeis and this is not surprising as the reports tell us of cultivation and farming, the development of which would have destroyed the papyrus which must have thrived in its earlier natural swampland.[215]

The other important fact that Rocchetta recorded about Bilbeis in 1599 was that it was at that time a garrison town. When he and his party arrived, they found a great number of soldiers who were heavily armed and the travellers were forbidden to wander through the town.[216] Rocchetta then relates the story of the conquest of Bilbeis in 1168 which may be found in several sources. We are told how Amaury, King of Jerusalem, crossed the desert with a large army in ten days and laid siege to this city, following his success by a brutal slaughter.

The Arab writers vocalized the name of this city as Bilbis, Bilbeis and Bulbeis and its Coptic name was Philbes.[217]

In 1879, the eminent Egyptologist Heinrich Brugsch drew attention to several passages from the ancient Egyptian inscriptions in which he recognized the name of Bilbeis, namely, pi-bairos/pi-bailos, quite possibly our early Byblos.[218] It is interesting to note that one of the texts he cites speaks of people pitching their tents in front of the city of pi-bailos, that is, outside its walls, just as many later travellers continued to do and as is recorded by Antonius Gonzales.[219] From a purely Egyptological context Heinrich Brugsch arrived at this sound interpretation which is confirmed by the writing of others on these customs.

Another passage quoted by Brugsch[220] and of great importance to us is from Papyrus Harris I, Plate 62a, line 2 in which the text refers to a temple or a town of Bast, the goddess of Bairos or Bailos, in the waters of Rē. We know that the cat goddess Bastet had her chief centre at Tell Basta (Zagaziq, see our fig. 12). The waters of Rē are acknowledged by all Egyptologists to have been situated in this vicinity, though we have no definite site for them. Brugsch thought that these waters could be a lake. We know for certain that this area abounded in natural springs and swampland in early times.

With regard to the abundance of water noted by the early travellers in the proximity of Bilbeis, we must add some further remarks by Aquilante Rocchetta, who was there, as we have said, in 1599. He describes leaving Catara (or Kattara, see our sketch map fig. 12) at one hour before daybreak en route for Bilbeis and arriving at dawn at the spring of the Pharaoh as the Arabs called it

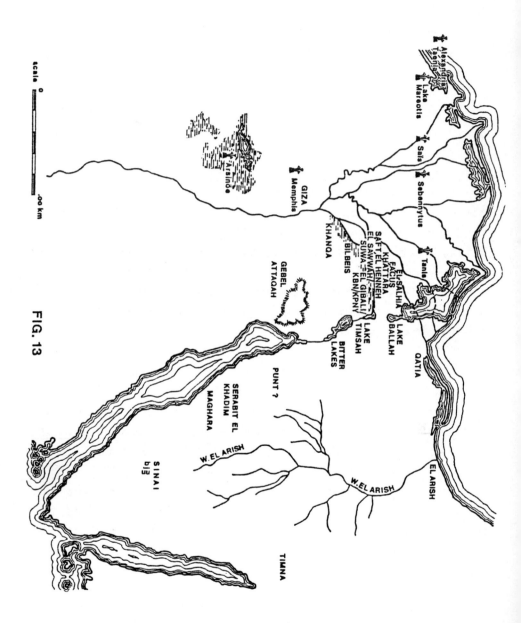

FIG. 13

in his day.[221]   He tells us that it was on the left
hand side of the road as he came south among the many
water reservoirs that he saw.   At this place there was a
fine portico with three arches and inside it there were
numerous rooms and a mosque.   Rocchetta described it as a
fine building, though not very large.   The story was told
in his day that the Pharaoh and his wife had come there
to relax in ancient times.

Besides the examples identified by Brugsch as
indicating the ancient name of Bilbeis, which we have
quoted here, there is an earlier example of this same
name in the Pyramid Texts, thus dating to the Old
Kingdom.   The Pyramid Text 456a refers to Sobek, as lord
of b3jrw.[222]   If Sobek, the crocodile god, was lord of
b3jrw it must have been a site where swampland
predominated in that early period rather than cultivated
land, because that is the natural environment of the
crocodile.   Both crocodiles and papyrus thrive in a
swampy environment.

x)   The Waters of Rēᶜ and Papyrus.

We quoted above a reference from the Papyrus Harris
telling us that Bairos or Bailos was situated in the
waters of Rēᶜ We have also quoted authoritative
statements that the name of Byblos is not an Indo-European
name.

It must be noted that the word papyrus also derives
from a non-Indo-European root.   Scholars have found this
word to have been used in the Greek only since the time of
Theophrastus.   H. G. Christesen[223] expressed the view
that it may be of Egyptian origin, coming from p3 pr
ᶜ3, originally meaning the great house.   The word
pharaoh is generally accepted to have come from the
expression pr ᶜ3 the great house.

In his inaugural lecture at University College, London, in 1947, Jaroslav Černý discussed a possible derivation for this word.[224] He said that in very late Bohairic (or Lower Egyptian) dialect of Coptic, papouro, though not actually attested, would mean that of the king. He emphasized that the Lower Egyptian or Bohairic form papouro is much closer to the Greek word than the form used in the Upper Egyptian or Sahidic dialect. Yet he saw a difficulty in the fact that the Egyptian and the Greek words were too similar, more than is usual in such cases. He pointed out another difficulty as well. How could the expression that of the king be applied to papyrus, unless it was assumed to be a royal monopoly? This discussion was continued by J. Vergote,[225] but without reaching any firm conclusions.

We have already referred to Brugsch's identification of pi-bairos/pi-bailos as present-day Bilbeis, which is undoubtedly the ancient Byblos in Egypt referred to by Ctesias and Stephen of Byzantium. Various popular forms of this name recorded by the early travellers have been given, as also the Coptic and Arabic forms.

I do not myself have the skills to offer a linguistic analysis of this material. I must leave this to the specialists. However, a little more can be said on a general level about this name and its associations.

There is abundant evidence, some of which has already been quoted, to show that the city of Bilbeis is situated on a site which was full of springs and reservoirs of water and plentiful in fish in ancient times. We know that fish will thrive in swampland and we also know that papyrus cannot live without it. If the word papyrus really has its origins in the Lower Egyptian dialect of Coptic, as Černý suggested,[226] then the expression that of the king or that which belongs to the ruler is an expression applying to the fabulous natural springs of that area rather than to the papyrus plant, which must have grown there abundantly in earlier times before farming practices were introduced into that area.

We have already quoted the report of Aquilante Rocchetta leaving Kattara at one hour before daybreak and arriving at dawn at a place called by the local inhabitants the spring of the pharaoh.[227] This is most likely to have been a lake commonly called until recent times Birket el Haggy el Beduin, namely the lake which refreshed the pilgrims on the way to their holy city (see our sketch map fig. 12). As we all know, Rē^c formed part of the title of the pharaohs of Egypt. It is therefore perfectly acceptable to equate the springs of the Pharaoh with the waters of Rē^c (see our sketch map fig. 12). Thus we can safely say that these waters extended at least between Bilbeis and the lake.

A further point must be made before leaving this discussion. The Assyrian Dictionary (1965) under B, p. 30 gives us the word bāʾilu meaning ruler, which occurs only in Middle Babylonian. Can it possibly be that in pi-bailos we have an exact foreign equivalent of the Egyptian expression that of the king, referring to some spectacularly abundant and excellent springs? If so, why do we have a Middle Babylonian word right on Egypt's borders during the New Kingdom?

This same section of The Assyrian Dictionary, p. 31 also gives us bāʾiru meaning fisherman or hunter. This alternative too would be very apt in this context, because it is a well-known fact that swampland is always teeming with animal life and is an ideal territory for the hunter as well as the fisherman.

We must therefore in due course study the possibility that pi-bailos or pi-bairos and papyrus may be derived from exactly the same root, though their development was different, because it occurred through separate channels.

xi)   References to a Town called The Papyrus City in the Egyptian Delta and its Possible Relationship to Papremis.

There are a number of references in the pharaonic texts to a town in the Egyptian delta called by the name the plant itself, papyrus, namely, p3 twf. The existence of this papyrus city in the Egyptian delta was noted and well documented by Alan Gardiner, initially in JEA 5 (1918), p. 186, note 1. In that article, Gardiner quoted from the Golenischeff Glossary no.38 (which is found on p. 198 of that same volume), where the town is listed after Buto and Tanis and before the fortress of t3rw, usually accepted as Sile (figs. 5, 12 and 13). It is unfortunate that t3rw has been equated with Sile as though it were a proven fact, which it is not. This renders any geographical discussion involving t3rw a speculative exercise.

Further examples of references to this papyrus city are given by Gardiner in his Ancient Egyptian Onomastica, Vol. II (1947), 201ff. It is important to note that the town determinative is always used with this expression so that it is clear that the texts are referring to a city. I believe we must disagree with Gardiner when he says that this expression with the town determinative can mean the papyrus marshes or the locality of the marshes rather than a city. We must disagree also with several other conclusions he offers in this respect, namely that the papyrus city can be equated with the sea of reeds of the Old Testament. It is possible that suph and twf are derived from the same root, but followed a different development, even within a few miles of each other. In time, it will become clear to us that the mixture of foreign people speaking different languages in the delta of Egypt produced different versions of some words which were in use simultaneously.

It seems that Gardiner's earlier discussion of the papyrus city was the more accurate one, when he adhered more closely to a literal reading for it, which took account of the town determinative which qualified it. It is written in this way in Papyrus Saillier I, 4:9; Papyrus Anastasi IV, 15:6; Papyrus Anastasi VIII, 3:4 and in the Golenischeff Glossary already mentioned above. The papyrus town is also mentioned in Speigelberg's Sagenkreis des König's Petubastis, Glossary, no. 582. This scholar placed this city further east than the others, though he gave no reason for doing it.

When we consider the statement we quoted above that the papyrus city is listed after Buto and Tanis but before the fortress of t3rw we have to remember that the Delta is not, even today, crossed with a satisfactory network of roads and canals that run from east to west or vice-versa. One may encounter serious difficulties even today in wishing to travel across the Delta because the main roads and the canals run from south to north. Until comparatively recent times, if one wished to travel from Alexandria to Damietta, the best way was by sea. Otherwise, by land and by canal it was necessary first to travel south and then northwards again when one came to the appropriate junction. George Sandys in 1611 tells us[228] that no traveller ever left Alexandria to travel directly eastwards. In his day, they all had to go to Cairo first. We are still very far from certain about the identity and duration of the ancient canals, though we are fortunate in having the detailed studies of Du Bois Aymé, published in conjunction with the Napoleonic Survey, followed by the analyses of Omar Tousson[229] of the geographical information available.

The existence of a town called p3 twf meaning the

papyrus city implies that

    a)   it was built on a sufficient height to be safe from the annual inundation;

    b)   it was an urban structure, presupposing boundaries and an administrative system, as the town determinative indicates;

    c)   it must have been situated in the middle of rich natural springs and thick swamps for such a name to have been given to it because papyrus will only grow in swampland.

It seems likely for the reasons which will follow that p3 twf may have been an alternative name for Bilbeis. According to the records we have already quoted, Bilbeis answers best to the characteristics we are given for p3 twf. But even more important is the evidence from the classical writers.

The passages we quoted above from Ctesias in Photius at the beginning of section ix) must be compared with the account by Herodotus iii, 12. In this chapter, Herodotus records the same events, namely the defeat of the Persians by Inaros the Libyan. However, although Ctesias describes this event as having taken place in a city called Byblos, Herodotus tells us that this same event took place at a city called Papremis.[230] Herodotus tells us (ii, 165) that this is also the name of the district or nome in which it was situated and he lists it together with Busiris, Sais, Chemmis and others, all in the delta of Egypt.

I am unable to discuss a possible derivation of the name of Papremis from a root which also produced papyrus. But one cannot help wondering at the similarity of these names in this identical historical context in which

Papremis must be equated to a Byblos in Egypt.

Several attempts have been made to identify Papremis from the linguistic point of view by J. Černý,[231] H. Altenmüller,[232] E. Bresciani,[233] A. B. Lloyd[234] and more recently by J. D. Ray[235] and H. de Meulenaere.[236] John Ray pointed out the fact that the name of Papremis is found in writings other than those of Herodotus, as for example in the P. Oxy. 1380, 22.[237]

None of these scholars, however, take into account the recorded fact that Papremis and Byblos in Egypt are two names for the same city, preserved in the Greek sources. One cannot but be surprised at the extent of the speculation upon which the linguistic discussion is based in some cases.

Herodotus tells us in ii, 71 that the hippopotamus was a sacred animal in the canton of Papremis. We know that swampland is the natural habitat of the hippopotamus, which had a special significance in the ancient world. It is also important to remember the other things which Herodotus tells us about Papremis. In ii, 59, we learn that the city held a great annual festival in honour of Ares or Mars, the god of war. In ii, 63-4, we are told that, besides the normal sacrifices and rites which took place in that city, a special event occurred. After sundown a god in a wooden box was moved by a group of men carrying clubs. At a certain point, these were challenged by another group also carrying clubs and then a violent fight took place. This association with Mars and a martial environment is in keeping with the character of a military fortress in an important strategic position. This fits the nature of the fortified city of Bilbeis as well as its geographical position and its history.

Further study may well confirm that we have the

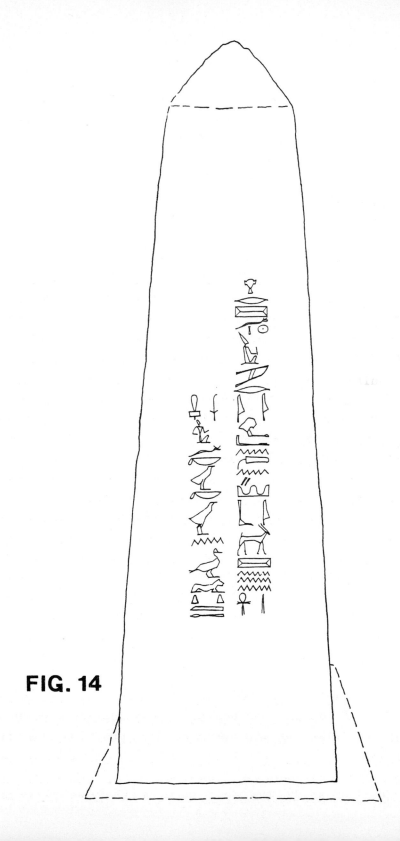

FIG. 14

Summary and Conclusion.

In the last hundred years, the interesting archaeological material which was found at Gebeil/Byblos was allowed too predominating a role in our assessment of the importance of that city throughout the history of the Near East.

This distortion in our interpretation of the facts was helped by many misconceptions from the Egyptological point of view. It was believed that the Egyptian $^{c}\underline{\breve{s}}$ meant _cedar_ and that it had to come from the Lebanon (sic). We now know that $^{c}\underline{\breve{s}}$ very probably meant _pine._ We also know that pine and oak grew abundantly along the northern boundaries of Egypt from pre-biblical times until our own day. Furthermore, there is now pollen evidence showing that _cedar_ thrived on the highlands of the Sahara, west of Egypt, probably into the early dynastic period. It may even be the case that it was the cedar seeds from these shores that were carried northwards by the sea currents, to produce cedar forests in the Lebanon in later times. It is a fact that the Nile silt found along the Palestinian coast carried Nile vegetation and pollens. There is no evidence that the Lebanese forests can have concerned Egypt at any stage in her history.

The equation of the Egyptian kbn/kpny with the Semitic gbl appears to be acceptable though it must be recognized that many chronological linguistic problems remain to be discussed in this respect. At the same time we must not equate either form of that name with Byblos because this is clearly derived from a different root.

A difficulty has always been recognized by careful scholars in deciding whether the ancient name of gbl found on so many Near Eastern documents can have been referring to Gebeil/Byblos in every case.

The identity of kbn/kpny in the Egyptian texts also raises problems, many of which have been discussed here. For over a decade I have been insisting that no evidence exists to justify saying that the ancient Egyptians ever went to sea and no scholar so far has been able to prove otherwise. Thus the very fact that the ancient Egyptians travelled to kbn/kpny by water in large transport vessels which were also used for going to the Sinai and to Punt means that this place was accessible by travelling on an inland water, such as the Wadi Tumilat. Apart from the evidence I offer here to identify the large ancient mound of El Gibali as the kbn/kpny of the Egyptian texts, my forthcoming reconsideration of the journey of Wenamun will finally, and scientifically, I hope, dispel any remaining doubts about the identification I propose here, albeit with an element of surprise.

Further complexity is added to this problem by the statements found in non-Egyptian texts affirming that there was a Gebal in Egypt as well as Gebeil/Byblos and also that there was a Byblos in Egypt as well as the northern one with the Greek name. But these two names of places stated to be in Egypt do not appear to be referring to the same site. I believe the Gebal in Egypt was El Gibali.

In addition to all this, we must note in passing that it is not Gebeil/Byblos, but the town of Gebala/Jebeleh, north of it, which has the large blocks of hewn stone along its harbour which are supposed to identify the biblical city of Gebal.

Three Greek historians make it clear in their accounts that the Byblos in Egypt and Papremis are one and the same city. However, if this is so, why the two names? This too is a complex problem, probably to be associated with its environmental characteristics.

There is plenty of evidence to show that the
historical variations of the writing of the name of
Bilbeis qualify it indisputably as the Byblos in Egypt.
This is further confirmed by the description of its
geographical position by Stephen of Byzantium, as being
between Bubastis (Tell Basta) and Heliopolis. The name
of Papremis which the historical accounts tell us was the
same city as Byblos in Egypt may be related to the
papyrus swampland in the middle of which the city of
Bilbeis was situated. It is noteworthy that the
Egyptians also had a city called p3 twf, meaning papyrus,
which may have been another name for Bilbeis in ancient
Egyptian. This would be all the more likely if the
pi-bairos/pi-bailos identified by Heinrich Brugsch as
Bilbeis in the ancient Egyptian were in fact of foreign
derivation. These words are attested in Middle
Babylonian.

It is probable that Gebeil/Byblos had no more
importance for ancient Egypt than any other centre with
which this country had contacts. Apart from the fact
that Gebeil/Byblos cannot ever have provided any timber
for Egypt at any stage in its history, it seems rather
that Gebeil/Byblos sought contact with Egypt for cultural
and perhaps religious reasons. We shall find it
increasingly clear that Egypt's neighbours moved very
close to her borders to bask in her culture and in her
religion. The evidence seems to indicate that they came
much closer to Egypt in a physical sense than we have
hitherto been willing to accept.

98

FOOTNOTES

1. A. Nibbi, "Some remarks on the Assumption of
    Ancient Egyptian Seagoing", Mariner's Mirror 65
    (1979), 201-208; AESEN, 25-7, 101, 176f; PEQ
    (1981), 89-99; "Ancient Egyptian Anchors: A Focus
    on the Facts", Mariner's Mirror 70 (1984), 247-266.

2. AESEN, 1-31.

3. ibid. See also "A Fresh Look at the Egyptian
    Environment of the Pharaonic Period", PEQ (1981),
    89-94; "On the Urgent Scientific Investigation of
    the Eastern Delta and Eastern Desert", Proceedings
    of the First International Congress of Egyptology,
    1976, ed. W. Reineke 1979; "Some Scientific
    Evidence for the Environment of Ancient Egypt",
    Proceedings of the Second International Congress of
    Egyptology, 1979. ed. J. Yoyotte, 1981.

4. AESEN, 17ff.

5. O. Bar-Yosef and J. L. Phillips, Prehistoric
    Investigations in Gebel Maghara, Northern Sinai,
    Qedem 7 (1977). Also in Paléorient 2 (1974).

6. This concept has been blindly accepted from scholar
    to scholar without question.

7. AESEN, 2-10.

8. Lines 80-85, Lichtheim I, 97f; W. Helck, Die Lehre
    für Meri-Ka-Re (1977).

9. "Quelques notes sur l'arbre ꜥš", Ann. Serv. 14
    (1916), 33-51.

10. AESEN, frontispiece, and 15f.

11. M. Har-El, "The Valley of the Craftsmen", PEQ 109,
    (1977), 75-86.

12. SPE passim and AESEN passim.

13. M. Botta and M. Flandrin, Monument de Nineve
    (1849), Vol. I, Plate 33.

14. Story of Wenamun, lines 2.35-2.40.

15. The Historical Geography of the Holy Land (1894),
    127f.

16. Pollen et Spores 3 (1961), 303-324.

17. Geographie des Alten Agyptens Vol. II (1858), 76f.

Footnotes (continued)

18. Brugsch at that time cited a map by Robinson but this site may now be seen in the Oxford Bible Atlas ed. H. G. May, p. 49 X 4, marked on our fig. 1 here.

19. F. W. Moon and H. Sadek, Topography and Geology of Northern Sinai, Ministry of Finance, Egypt, Petroleum Research Bulletin no. 10 (1921), p. 11 and Plate II.

20. O. Bar-Yosef and others, Prehistoric Investigations in Gebel Maghara, Northern Sinai, Qedem 7 (1977); also Paléorient 2 (1974), 483f.

21. H. Halm, Ägypten nach den mamlukischen Lehensregistern II (1982), p. 642 and map no. 30.

22. Asien und Europa (1893), 196-204.

23. Exterior North Wall of Great Hall, PM II, 54; Wreszinski, Atlas II, Plates 34 and 39.

24. AESEN, chapter 1; also Nibbi in PEQ (1981), 89-99.

25. S. I. Saad and S. Sami, "Studies in Spores Content of the Nile Delta Deposits (Berenbal Region)", Pollen et Spores 9 (1967), 467-503. See also Martine Rossignol in Pollen et Spores 3 (1961), 303-324.

26. "Eine Reise nach Phönizien", ZAS 38 (1900), 1-14.

27. ZAS 45 (1908-9), 7-16.

28. Ann. Serv. 16 (1916), 33-51.

29. See note 7 above; also "Some Evidence from Scientists Indicating the Vegetation of Lower and Middle Egypt during the Pharaonic Period", L'Egyptologie en 1979 Tome I (CRNS, 1982), ed. J. Yoyotte, 247-254.

30. AEO I, pp. 140, 142ff, 150, 172f.

31. Beziehungen 21ff, 267f, 272f, 374ff.

32. Les guerres d'Amosis (1971), 96ff, 161, 171, 192, 201.

33. AESEN cit. chapter 1; also Nibbi, "Some Remarks on the Assumption of Ancient Egyptian Seagoing", Mariner's Mirror 65 (1979), 201-8; Furthermore Nibbi, "Ancient Egyptian Anchors: A Focus on the Facts", Mariner's Mirror 70 (1984), 247-266. On the question of the so-called port on the Red Sea,

see Nibbi, " Some Remarks on the Two Monuments from Mersa Gawasis", Ann. Serv. (1981), 69-74.

34. The problem relating to Gebeil/Byblos and Egypt is a complex one, compounded by the assumptions that have been built up around it over the last hundred years.

35. G. A. Reisner and M. B. Reisner, "Inscribed Monuments from Gebel Barkal", ZAS 69 (1933), 34.

36. In the earliest discussions on Djahy scholars naturally placed Djahy immediately upon Egypt's boundaries. However, they understood these to be the same boundaries as today and not the natural boundary where the water of the Nile divided into many streams.

37. cit. 90-102, 119-121, 125ff, 200f.

38. ibid. 91.

39. ibid.

40. ibid. 92f.

41. As we have no proof for these identifications, they cannot be used to identify other places in any argument.

42. We are still very far from understanding who the Fenkhu were because we accept a priori that they are the Phoenicians, even though no satisfactory definition of these people exists either.

43. Oriental Institute, University of Chicago, Medinet Habu, Plate 31. See also Plate 78, line 5.

44. SPE, chapters 1 and 2; also Nibbi, "The Chief Obstacle to Understanding the Wars of Ramesses III".

45. The Satrap Stela indicates beyond dispute that the Haunebut were settled in the vicinity of Alexandria, see Nibbi "Rakotis on the Shore of the Great Green of the Haunebut", GM 69 (1983), 69-80.

46. There is abundant evidence in the published texts that sht-j3m should be associated with Kom el Hisn (see fig. 4 here). See AESEN cit. 126-134.

47. See notes 7, 18 and 11 above.

48. ibid.

Footnotes (continued)

49.   Review of AESEN in PEQ (1983), 77-79.

50.   Chr. d'Egypte 58 (1983), 115f.

51.   GM 64 (1983), 7.

52.   Voyage d'un Egyptien en Syrie, 157-160.   This
       Papyrus, Anastasi I was later presented in a
       hieroglyphic text, with translation, by A. H.
       Gardiner, Hieratic Texts (1911). We shall return
       to look more closely at this name later in a
       special section.

53.   ZAS 45 (1908), 7-11. This form is also found in
       later times as we discuss below.

54.   See John Gwyn Griffiths, De Iside et Osiride (1970)
       on Plutach's Chapters 13 and 15. Plutarch tells us
       that the ornate box carrying Osiris went down the
       river towards the sea by way of the Tanitic mouth
       "which the Egyptians still call, because of this,
       hateful and abominable". This box was cast up by
       the sea (sic) in the land of Byblos. We cannot be
       sure about Plutarch's sources for this story, but
       one thing is certain. This version of the myth can
       have arisen only after the name of Byblos was given
       to the city, wherever it was, and not before that
       time.

55.   A translation may be found in H. A. Strong, The
       Syrian Goddess (1913), 45-47. There is a great
       deal more interference in his account where a head
       is said to have floated into Byblos each year.
       Lucian compares the Adonis legend with that of
       Osiris. Lucian reports on an important temple
       dedicated to a goddess on this site. There is a
       very ancient tradition in the Mediterranean and
       Aegean for the veneration of goddesses rather than
       gods and there are a number of ancient temples
       dedicated to female deities along the Near Eastern
       coast. But these goddesses cannot be closely
       identified in many cases. A Byblos coin reproduces
       a shrine to a goddess.

56.   Chabas, op. cit. 158f.

57.   Mission de Phénicie (1864).

58.   Asien und Europa (1893), 188-191.

59.   ibid. 189f.

Footnotes (continued)

60. René Dussaud simply accepted the equivalence of these terms in his studies in Syria 5 (1924), 388f and Syria 8 (1927), 217f. A more recent study concerning this name begins by accepting, not explaining, this equivalence: see W. Weidmüller, "Der Buchstabe 'K'", Mélanges de l'Université de Saint-Joseph 45 (1969), 277-293.

61. Sphinx 11 (1908), 201-205.

62. Notes on the Story of Sinuhe (1916), 23. See pp. 21-23 and 166-167.

63. H. Gauthier, Dictionnaire géographique (1925-31). See Vol. K, 197-8. Here Gauthier quotes an example from Daressy where this name is written with the town determinative and associated by Daressy with the third Lower Egyptian nome. But it is treated by Gauthier as unrelated to kbn/kpny as a foreign place.

64. Cat. no. 3036, Inventory no. 5544. R. V. Lanzone, Dizionario di Mitologia Egizia (1882), cccxxiv.

65. Enciclopedia Italiana Treccani, entry Biblo.

66. Vetus Testamentum 1 (1951), 130-1.

67. Minos N.S. 16 (1977), 7-11.

68. ibid. 8f.

69. 1968-1980.

70. Studi Etruschi 6 (1932), 243-260.

71. ibid. 251f. It is interesting to note that Devoto believed this root to have given rise to nouns such as populus/publicus and to the personal names Publius/Popilius and Fufluns, the Etruscan god.

72. ibid. 252f. There is, of course, the possibility that the ancient hills or mounds of earth have been removed in the course of time to make way for arable land, as is the case in the Egyptian Delta.

73. ibid. 253.

74. G. Alessio, Studi Etruschi 18 (1944), 122-3.

75. Devoto, op. cit. 249f.

76. ibid. 250f.

Footnotes (continued)

77. ibid. 251f.

78. ibid. 260.

79. Emprunts Sémitiques en Grec (1967), 101-7.

80. ibid. 101f.

81. ibid. 104.

82. SPE 12 and 52.

83. L'Industrie de papyrus (1934); Papyrus in Classical Antiquity (1974).

84. op. cit. 1974, 115. See also p. 85.

85. "Did Papyrus Grow in the Aegean?", Athens Annals of Archaeology 9 (1977), 89-95.

86. Lewis, op. cit. 1974, p. 12 note 12; also 104f and 116ff.

87. ibid. 117.

88. ibid. 104f.

89. ibid. 86ff.

90. op. cit. see note 79 above, 104f.

91. L. A. Knudtzon, Die El-Amarna Tafeln (1915), p. 1574 sets out all the variations in the writing of this name. Also S. Mercer, The Tell El-Amarna Tablets (1939), p. 836, Excursus VI. For the letters found after those dates, see A. F. Rainey, El Amarna Tablets 359-379 (1970). As many as 73 of these letters are written to and from Gubla, 64 of them being correspondence with Rib-Addi. The identity of this city has always been assumed to be Gebeil/Byblos, though there is no positive evidence for this.

92. M. N. Adler, Itinerary of Benjamin of Tudela (1907).

93. ibid. 16f.

94. Syria 7 (1926), 247-256.

95. "Fouilles de Byblos", Bulletin du Musée de Beyrouth, 1948-1959.

96. Geog. 16.2.18.

Footnotes (continued)

97. British War Office, <u>Syria, Geographical Handbook
    Series</u> (1943), <u>Gebeil/Byblos,</u> 319f and Plate 131;
    <u>Gabala,</u> pp. 315 and 414, and Plate 43. This work
    describes as a port the two rows of buildings
    founded on the existing reefs, which stretch out as
    arms into the sea at Gebeil/Byblos. But these
    buildings belong to our own era and envelop a space
    which is far too small to serve as a harbour, even
    for the smaller ancient vessels. See our fig. 6.

98. <u>A Description of the East and Some Other Countries</u>
    (1745), Part I, Vol. 2, see 97f for "Esbele" Byblos
    and 198f for the town of <u>Gabala</u> which was called in
    his day <u>Jebilee.</u> Pococke also mentions an
    important harbour in the second town, as well as an
    amphitheatre remaining from classical times, but no
    port or harbour is described for Gebeil/Byblos,
    though he stated his acceptance of the belief that
    this must be the ancient biblical city.

99. C. Schefer, <u>Sefer Nameh, Relation des Voyages de
    Nassiri Khosrau</u> (translation 1881), 46f.

100. Ann M. H. Ehrich, <u>Early Pottery of the Jebeleh
     Region</u> (1939), <u>Mem. of the Amer. Philos. Soc.</u> Vol.
     13, 120f.

101. W. F. Albright, "The Eighteenth Century Princes of
     Byblos and the Chronology of Middle Bronze", <u>BASOR</u>
     176 (1964), p. 40 and note 6.

102. Ch. Clermont-Ganneau, <u>Recueil d'archéologie
     orientale</u> VI, Plate II and p. 74. Also Dussaud,
     <u>Syria</u> V (1924), Plate XLII and pp. 145f.

103. ibid. p. 145. However, see P. Montet, <u>Byblos et
     l'Egypte,</u> Texte (1928). 54 and 57.

104. <u>Syria</u> V (1924), 145, note 1.

105. <u>Comptes-Rendus des Séances de l'Année 1903,
     Académie des Inscriptions et Belles-Lettres,</u> pp. 91
     and 378-383.

106. <u>Recueil d'archéologie orientale</u> VI (1905), 74-78 and
     Plate II. See also Libzbarski, <u>Ephemeris für
     Semit. Epig.</u> II, 167 who accepts a <u>Gebal in Egypt.</u>

107. cit. note 105.

108. cit. note 101 above.

109. cit. note 103 above.

Footnotes (continued)

110. Kanaänaische und Aramäische Inschriften (1962), no. 5, 7f.

111. Textbook of Syrian Semitic Inscriptions, Vol. III, Phoenician Inscriptions (1982), no. 7.

112. cit. pp. 7f.

113. J. G. Février, "L'Inscription d'Abiba'al, roi de Byblos", Africa, Inst. Nat. d'Arch. et d'Art de Tunis (1966), 13-17.

114. Molk als Opferbegriff (1935), 29-30.

115. Dussaud, cit. (1924), 145.

116. K. Kuhlmann, Der Thron im Alten Ägypten (1977), 52ff.

117. pp. 479 and 553, note 4.

118. They are not illustrated in his publication.

119. Rec. de Travaux, XVII, 14f.

120. Sphinx XVI (1912), 14.

121. Dussaud, cit. (1925), 109.

122. ibid. 101-117.

123. ibid. 117, postscript.

124. cit. introductory chapter.

125. ibid. p. 129.

126. ibid. p. 103.

127. ibid. p. 104. See also N. Jidejian, Byblos Through the Ages (1968), 16f.

128. cit. p. 104.

129. ibid. p. 105.

130. See notes 1 and 3 above.

131. See notes 9 and 10 above.

132. cit. p. 106.

133. ibid. p. 108f.

106

Footnotes (continued)

134. ibid. p. 110f.

135. Levant IV (1972), 98-110.

136. Dunand, Fouilles II (1), 196f.

137. Dunand, Fouilles I, 104, no. 1551.

138. ibid. 185, no. 2905.

139. Montet, Byblos et l'Egypte, 155, no. 610.

140. ibid. p. 157, no. 611.

141. ibid. p. 159, no. 614.

142. ibid. p. 165, no. 168.

143. Fouilles II (2), 644ff.

144. ibid.

145. Montet, Kêmi XVI (1962), 89f.

146. ibid. 96.

147. ibid. 89f. Montet compared this inscription with the one on the Obelisk no. 15 from Tanis. W. H. F. Kuykendall finds in it a close similarity with the Middle Kingdom stelae from Serabit El Khadim in the Sinai in Egyptian Religious Activity in Palestine and Syria During the Third and Second Millennium B.C. Ph.D. John Hopkins University, 1966, 48f.

148. Dunand, Fouilles I, pp. 54-6 and Plate XXVII.

149. PM VI, 385.

150. Montet, Byblos et l'Egypte, pp. 48f and Plate XXXIV.

151. ibid. p. 225 and p. 227.

152. Fouilles I, pp. 53f, 56, 93 and 339.

153. Lexikon, entry Meer. See also comments by Nibbi in GM 58 (1982); also Nibbi, "Ancient Egyptian Anchors: A Focus on the Facts", Mariner's Mirror 70 (1984), 247-266.

154. R. Eisler, Die kenitischen Weihinschriften der Hyksos (1919), 138.

155. A. Mallon, "Les Hébreux en Egypte", Orientalia 3

Footnotes (continued)

(Old Series, 1921), 18f. He found it odd that
Sinuhe should arrive so quickly in kbn/kpny if this
was Gebeil/Byblos. Nor were any places mentioned
between the point of his departure and his arrival
in kbn/kpny.

156. Orientalia 46 (1977), p. 135, note 14.

157. ZAS 38 (1900), 1-18; ZAS 45 (1908), 7-35.

158. Byblos et l'Egypte (1928).

159. Dussaud simply accepted the equivalence of these
terms in his studies. See Syria V (1924), 388f;
ibid. VIII (1927), 217f. A more recent study
concerning this name also begins by accepting, not
explaining, this equivalence: see W. Weidmüller,
"Der Buchstabe 'K'", Mélanges de l'Université de
Saint-Joseph 45 (1969), 277-293.

160. AEO I, pp. 142, 150, 182.

161. AESEN, chapter 1; also Nibbi in PEQ (1981), 89-99.

162. M. Harel, The Route of the Exodus, A Geographical
Survey (1976), Diss. University of New York, 1965.

163. AESEN, 2f.

164. See Geoffrey Martin's comments on the Egyptian
objects from Kition in JEA 67 (1981), 203f.

165. C. F-A. Schaeffer, Ugaritica III (1939), 20f.

166. T. Dothan, Excavations at the Cemetery of Deir
El-Balah (Qedem X, 1979).

167. Dictionnaire géographique, see K 197f.

168. See note 157 above.

169. AESEN, chapters 5 and 6.

170. Urk. I, 134, 15.

171. ZAS 42 (1905), 109f.

172. Urk. IV, 707.

173. D. Paton, Egyptian Records of Travel in Western
Asia, Vol. III (2), p. 89.

174. Notes on the Story of Sinuhe (1916), pp. 21-23 and
166-7.

108

Footnotes (continued)

175. J. J. Clère, <u>Mélanges Syriens offerts à René Dussaud</u> (1939), 827-840.

176. See note 139 above.

177. <u>AESEN</u>, 175f.

178. <u>AEO</u> II, pp. 156, 162, 195.

179. ed. S. Sauneron (1971), 161f. This place was in the vicinity of the Matariyah of today.

180. J. Couyat and P. Montet, <u>Les inscriptions hiéroglyphiques et hiératiques du Ouadi Hammamat,</u> <u>MIFAO</u> 34 (1912), 81ff. See comments by Nibbi in <u>GM</u> 17 (1975), 39-44.

181. V. Denon, <u>Voyages dans la Basse et la Haute Egypte</u> Tome II (1807), Appendix p. ccxiv, quotes this as meaning "the dome of justice" while a footnote corrects this by saying the name means simply "dome". It is possible, however, that the name goes back much further into ancient Egyptian times.

182. <u>AESEN</u> 73ff.

183. "Some Remarks on Ass and Horse in Ancient Egypt and the Absence of the Mule", <u>ZAS</u> 106 (1979), pp. 148-168.

184. <u>Urk. I</u>, 140f.

185. <u>Urk. I</u>, 131f.

186. See note 180 above.

187. <u>AESEN</u>, chapters 6 and 7.

188. Our fig. 13 shows how, for different reasons in each case, all three places, namely <u>bj3</u> indicating the <u>Sinai</u>, <u>Punt</u> indicating the incense-tree bearing area and <u>kbn/kpnj</u> indicating either a place called <u>Gebeil</u> or a place where a great quantity of incense was burnt - all lay in the same easterly direction from Egypt.

189. S. Allam, <u>Beiträge zum Hathorkult,</u> (1963), 132 and 142.

190. <u>AESEN</u>, 103f.

191. Dunand, <u>Fouilles</u> I, 200 and Plate CXXV; also Montet, <u>Kêmi</u> XVI (1962), 88.

Footnotes (continued)

192. Dunand, Fouilles I, 417f.

193. R. Lanzone, Dizionario Mitologico p. 899 and Plate 324. G. Maspéro, Rec. Travaux II, 120; A. Erman, ZAS 42 (1905), 109.

194. Montet, Byblos et l'Egypte, Texte, 42f.

195. W. Schenkel, Die Bewässerungsrevolution im Alten Ägypten (1979), 22f and 59f; also E. Endesfelder in ZAS 106 (1979), 37-51.

196. Description de l'Egypte, ed. Panckoucke (1829), text vol. 5, 146-154.

197. G. Posener, "Le canal du Nil à la Mer Rouge avant les Ptolomées", Chronique d'Egypte 13 (1938), 259-273; see also A. Lloyd in JEA 58 (1972), 268-279 and in JHS 95 (1975), 45-61.

198. Nibbi, Mariner's Mirror (1984), 261f.

199. B. Rothenberg, Timna (1972), chapter 5.

200. Gardiner, Peet and Černý, The Inscriptions of Sinai, (1955), Part II, Chapter V and Plates XVI ff.

201. AESEN, chapters 5 and 6 consider all the documentary references for Punt and conclude that the only possible site for it was in the central, western Sinai, when all the evidence is taken into account.

202. Review by K. A. Kitchen in Palestine Exploration Quarterly 1983, 77-79.

203. F. W. König, Die Persiker des Ctesias von Knidos (1972), 13f; J. Gilmore, The Fragments of the Persika of Ktesias (1888), 160-166.

204. Stephen of Byzantium, Ethnica, ed. A. Meineke, 1859.

205. W. Schenkel, Die Bewässerungsrevolution im Alten Ägypten (1979); E. Endesfelder, "Zur Frage der Bewässerung im Pharaonischen Ägypten", ZAS 106 (1979), 37-51.

206. E. N. Adler, Jewish Travellers (1930), 176.

207. Voyages en Egypte des années 1589, 1590 et 1591, ed. C. Burri, N. Sauneron et P. Bleser (1971), folio 44.

110

208. M. Bietak, "Avaris and Piramesses", Proceedings of the British Academy (London) Vol. LXV (1979), 225-289.

209. Voyage en Egypte 1482-3, ed. A. Bauwens-Préaux (1976), folio 137.

210. It was called in mediaeval and possibly earlier times "the gateway to Syria", Wiet et Maspéro, 45f.

211. Villes et Légendes (1974), 143f.

212. As, for example, Belon du Mesnil and many others.

213. Voyage en Egypte, 1665-6, ed. C. Libois (1977), folio 623.

214. Voyages en Egypte, 1597-1601 ed. S. Sauneron (1974), folios 303-306.

215. An artist in Zagazig told me that, as far back as he could remember, he had always picked papyrus in swamps to the east of the city, about 12 kilometres away.

216. Rochetta, cit. see note 214 above.

217. Wiet and Maspéro, cit. p. 45f. These scholars tell us that Bilbeis was a fortified town surrounded by a ditch during the Middle Ages. Situated as it was on the regular route of travellers and invaders of Egypt, it was the subject of many sieges by foreign armies during its history. These scholars list a number of sieges dating to the Middle Ages and earlier and they emphasize not unnaturally, as did also Blochet (Histoire d'Egypte, 258), that a great deal of attention was always paid to this city's fortifications. See also E. M. Quatremère, Mémoires sur l'Egypte I, 319, and E. Amélineau, La géographie de l'Egypte à l'epoque copte (1893), 177, 255, 330, 333-5, 497.

218. Dictionnaire géographique, pp. 77 and 197.

219. See note 213 above.

220. cit. p. 197.

221. See not 214 above.

222. K. Sethe, Die altägyptischen Pyramidentexte 2 vols. (1908); S. Mercer, The Pyramid Texts 4 vols (1952).

Footnotes (continued)

223. *Orientalische Literaturzeitung* XLI (1938), columns 204-5.

224. *Paper and Books in Ancient Egypt.*

225. *Mélanges Grégoire* 3 (1951), 414-416.

226. op. cit.

227. See note 214 above.

228. Edition *IFAO* ED. O. V. Volkoff (1973), folio 107.

229. *Mémoire sur les anciennes branches du Nil*, *MIFAO* IV (1922), Plate I.

230. Much has been written on *Papremis* and it is not possible to summarize all the speculation with regard to an identification of this town.

231. *Archiv Orientalni* 20 (1952), 86-89.

232. *JEOL* 18 (1964), 271-279.

233. *Studi Classici e Orientali* 21 (1972), 299-303.

234. *Herodotus, Book II*, 1-98; also *Etudes préliminaires aux religions orientales dans l'empire romain* (*EPRO*) 43 (1976), 270-272.

235. *GM* 45 (1981), 58-61.

236. Entry *Papremis* in *Lexikon für Ägyptologie.*

237. cit. 59.

238. *Tell Basta* (1957), 123f.

239. W. M. FLinders Petrie and J. G. Duncan, *Hyksos and Israelite Cities* (1906).

240. E. Naville, *The Mound of the Jew* (1887), 22f.

241. cit. 45ff.

242. *PM* IV, 55-56.

243. Nibbi, review of *Excavations in Egypt*, ed. T. G. H. James (1982), in *Biblioteca Orientalis* XL (1983), 71.

BIBLIOGRAPHY

Nina Jidejian's <u>Byblos Through the Ages</u> (1968) has a complete bibliography of the classical and mediaeval writers about this city. For this reason I do not list any here except where they occur directly in my discussion. On the other hand, Muntaha Saghieh's <u>Byblos in the Third Millennium</u> (1983) contains a full archaeological bibliography of the finds relating to Byblos. Between them, therefore, these authors offer us as complete a bibliography on Byblos as we can hope for. My own list here is for quick reference to the work directly connected with my discussion, with the addition of one or two titles from our Egyptological area of study.

Albright, William F.

"An Indirect Synchronism Between Egypt and Mesopotamia ca. 1730 B.C.", <u>BASOR</u> No. 99 (1945), 9-17.

"A Lycian at the Byblian Court", <u>BASOR</u>, 155 (1959), 31-41. <u>The Archaeology of Palestine</u>, Harmondsworth, (1960).

"Abram the Hebrew: A New Archaeological Interpretation", <u>BASOR</u>, 163 (1961) 36ff.

"The Chronology of Middle Bronze I (Early Bronze - Middle Bronze)", <u>BASOR</u>, 168 (1962) 36ff.

"Further Light on the History of Middle Bronze Byblos", <u>BASOR</u>, 179 (1965) 38ff.

"Remarks on the Chronology of Early Bronze IV - Middle Bronze IIA in Phoenicia and Syria-Palestine", <u>BASOR</u>, 184 (1966) 26ff.

"Some Remarks on the Archaeological Chronology of Palestine before about 1500 B.C.", <u>Chronologies</u> (1967) 47ff.

"The Excavation of tell Beit Mirsim IA: The Bronze Age Pottery of the Fourth Campaign", <u>BASOR</u>, XVII (1933) 55ff.

Bibliography (continued)

"The High Place in Ancient Palestine", <u>Vetus Testmentum</u>, Supplement IV (1957) 242ff.

Chéhab, Maurice   "Un trésor d'orfèvrerie syro-égyptien", BMB I (1937), 7-21.

Contenau, G.   <u>La civilisation phénicienne.</u> Paris: Payot, 1949.

Daressy, G.   "Une Statue de Saft-El-Henneh", <u>Ann. Serv.</u> XI (1919).

Dever, W. G.   "The Middle Bronze I Period in Syria and Palestine", NEATC, New York (1970) 132ff.

Dunand, Maurice   <u>Byblos, son histoire, ses ruines, ses légendes,</u> Beyrouth, (1963).

<u>Fouilles de Byblos,</u> I and II. Paris: Librarie Orientaliste Paul Geuthner, (1939).

"Rapport préliminaire sur les fouilles de Byblos en 1948", BMB IX (1949), 53-64.

"Rapport préliminaire sur les fouilles de Byblos en 1949", BMB IX (1949), 65-74.

"Rapport préliminaire sur les fouilles de Byblos en 1950", BMB XII (1955), 7-12.

"Rapport préliminaire sur les fouilles de Byblos en 1951", BMB XII (1955), 13-20.

"Rapport préliminaire sur les fouilles de Byblos en 1952", BMB XII (1955), 21-23.

"Rapport préliminaire sur les fouilles de Byblos en 1954", BMB XIII (1956), 73-78.

"Rapport préliminaire sur les fouilles de Byblos en 1955", BMB XIII (1956), 81-86.

114

Bibliography (continued)

"Rapport préliminaire sur les fouilles de Byblos en 1957", BMB XVI (1964), 69-73.

"Rapport préliminaire sur les fouilles de Byblos en 1958", BMB XVI (1964), 75-79.

"Rapport préliminaire sur les fouilles de Byblos en 1959", BMB XVI (1964), 81-85.

"La sixième campagne de fouilles de Byblos", Syria IX (1928), 1-5, second article 173-186.

"La septième campagne de fouilles de Byblos", Syria X (1929), 206-216.

Dussaud, René — "Les inscriptions phéniciennes du tombeau d'Ahiram, roi de Byblos", Syria V (1924), 135-155.

"Dédicace d'une statue d'Osorkon par Elibaal, roi de Byblos", Syria VI (1925), 101-110.

"Inscription phénicienne de Byblos de l'epoque romaine", Syria VI (1925), 269-173.

"Le sanctuaire phénicien de Byblos d'après Benjamin de Tudèle", Syria VII (1927), 247-256.

"Les quatre campagnes de fouilles de M. Pierre Montet à Byblos", Syria XI (1930), 164-187.

Ehrich, A. M. H. — Early Pottery of the Jebeleh Region, Memoirs of the American Philosophical Society, XIII, (1939).

Ehrich, R. W., ed. — Chronologies in Old World Archaeology, (1967).

Bibliography (continued)

Emery, W. B.   Great Tombs of the First
                                Dynasty, vol. I, (1949).

                                Great Tombs of the First
                                Dynasty, vols. II, III,
                                (1954, 1958).

Fischer, H. G.   Inscriptions from the Coptite
                                Nome, (1964).

Goedicke, Hans   "A Cylinder Seal of a Ruler
                                of Byblos of the Third
                                Millennium", Mitteilungen des
                                Deutchen Archaeologischen
                                Instituts Abteilung Kairo XIX
                                (1963), 1-5.

                                "The Cylinder Seal of a Ruler
                                of Byblos Reconsidered",
                                Journal of the American
                                Center in Egypt V (1966),
                                19-21.

Hari, R.   Horemheb et la reine
                                Moutnedjemet ou la fin d'une
                                dynastie, (1964).

Helck, H. W.   Die Beziehungen Ägyptens zu
                                Vorderasien im 2. und 3.
                                Jahrtausend v. Chr. (1962 and
                                1971).

                                Geschichte des alten Agypten,
                                (1968).

Hornung, E.   Untersuchungen zur
                                Chronologie und Geschichte
                                des Neuen Reiches, (1964).

Kantor, H.   "The Early Relations of Egypt
                                with Asia", JNES, 1 (1942)
                                174ff.

                                "The Relative Chronology of
                                Egypt and its Foreign
                                Correlations before the Late
                                Bronze Age", Chronologies
                                (1967) 1ff.

Kenyon, K.   "Some notes on the Early and
                                Middle Bronze Age Strata of
                                Megiddo", EI V (1958) 51ff.

Bibliography (continued)

<table>
<tr><td></td><td><u>Excavations at Jericho I and II,</u> (1960, 1964).</td></tr>
</table>

Excavations at Jericho I and II, (1960, 1964).

"Syria and Palestine c. 2160-1780 B.C.", CAH2, 29, parts V-VII, (1965) 38ff.

"Archaeology in the Holy Land, 3rd. edn., (1970).

Kitchen, K. A.   "Byblos, Egypt and Mari in the Early Second Millennium B.C.", Orientalia XXXVI N.S., (1967) 39ff.

Knudtzon, J. A.   Die El-Amarna Tafeln, (1907-1915).

Kuykendall, W. H. F.   Egyptian Religious Activity in Palestine and Syria During the Third and Second Millennia B. C., Ph. D., John Hopkins University, 1966.

Lloyd, A.   Herodotus, Book II, Introduction, (1975).

                          Herodotus, Book II, Commentary 1-98, (1976).

Martin, G.   "A New Prince of Byblos", JNES 27, 1968.

                          "A Ruler of Byblos of the Second Intermediate Period", Berytus XVIII, (1969).

Martin, M.   "A Preliminary Report after Re-Examination of the Byblian Inscriptions", Orientalia 30, (1961).

                          "Revision and Reclassification of the Proto-Byblian Signs", Orientalia 31, (1961).

Mercer, Samuel B.   The Tell-el-Amarna Tablets, 2 vols., (1939).

Montet, Pierre   Byblos et l'Egypte, Quatre campagnes de fouilles à

Bibliography (continued)

Gebeil 1921, 1922, 1923, 1924, (1928).

"Dépots d'offrandes à Byblos et a Tod", Kêmi XVI (1962), 89-90.

"La IVe dynastie à Byblos", Kêmi XVI (1962), 86-89.

"Quatre nouvelles inscriptions hiéroglyphiques trouvées à Byblos", Kêmi XVII (1964), 61-68.

"Le pays de Negaou près de Byblos et son dieu", Syria IV (1923), 180-182.

"Un Egyptien roi de Byblos sous la XIIe Dynastie", Syria VIII (1927), 85-92.

"Sur quelques objets provenant de Byblos", Syria X (1929), 12-15.

Moorey, P. R. S.
        and Parr, P. J. eds.   Archaeology in the Levant, Essays for Kathleen Kenyon, (1978).

Mouterde, R.   "Date des inscriptions forestières d'Hadrien au Liban", Mélanges de la Faculté Orientale de l'Université Saint-Joseph XXV (1942-1943), 41-47.

Movers, F. C.   Die Phönizier, (1856).

Naville, Eduard   "Le vase a parfum de Byblos", Syria III (1922), 291-295.

The City of Onias and the Mound of the Jew, (1890).

Neghbi, Ora and
        Moskowitz, S.   "The Foundation Deposits or Offering Deposits of Byblos", BASOR 184, (1966), 21-26.

Bibliography (continued)

Nelson, Harold H.   "Fragments of Egyptian Old
                           Kingdom Stone Vases from
                           Byblos", Berytus I (1934),
                           19-22.

Newberry, Percy E.   "A Middle Kingdom Mayor of
                           Byblos", JEA XIV (1928), p.
                           109.

Nibbi, A.   Ancient Egypt and Some
                           Eastern Neighbours (Noyes
                           Press, New Jersey, 1981).

                           "Ancient Egyptian Anchors: A
                           Focus on the Facts",
                           Mariner's Mirror 70 (1984).

                           "The Chief Obstacle to
                           Understanding the Wars of
                           Ramesses III", GM 59 (1982).

                           "A Fresh Look at the Ancient
                           Egyptian Environment", PEQ
                           (1981).

                           "The Great Tombos
                           Inscription: Some
                           Geographical Notes", JARCE 13
                           (1976).

                           "A Note on the Lexikon Entry:
                           Meer", GM 58 (1982).

                           "Rakotis on the Shore of the
                           Great Green of the Haunebut",
                           GM 69 (1983).

                           "The rhj.-t-people as
                           Permanent Foreigners in
                           Ancient Egypt", Proceedings
                           of the Fourth International
                           Colloquium of Pharaonic Law,
                           ed. I. Harari.

                           The Sea Peoples and Egypt,
                           (Noyes Press, New Jersey,
                           1975).

                           "A Scientific Challenge to K.
                           A. Kitchen", GM 64 (1983).

                           "Shipwreck on the Waters of
                           the Nile", GM 16 (1975).

Bibliography (continued)

"Some Remarks on Ass and Horse in Ancient Egypt and the Absence of the Mule", ZAS 106 (1979).

"Some Remarks on the Assumption of Ancient Egyptian Sea-going", Mariner's Mirror 65 (1979).

"Some Remarks on the Two Stelae from the Wadi Gasus", JEA 62 (1976).

"Some Remarks on the Two Monuments from the Wadi Gawasis", Ann. Serv. 64 (1981).

"The Wadi Tumilat, ATIKA and MW-QD," GM 16 (1975).

"YM and the Wadi Tumilat", GM 15 (1975).

Pauly's Real-Encyclopädie — (1899). Entry: Byblos, pp. 1099-1102.

Pillet, Maurice — "Le temple de Byblos", Syria VIII (1927), 105-112.

Posener, G. — Princes et pays d'Asie et de Nubie, (1940).

"Sur les inscriptions pseudo-hiéroglyphiques de Byblos", Mélanges de l'Université de Saint-Joseph 45, (1969).

Pritchard, James B. ed. — Ancient Near Eastern Texts Relating to the Old Testament, (1955).

Rawlinson, George — History of Phoenicia, London, (1889).

Redford, D. — History and Chronology of the Eighteenth Dynasty of Egypt, (1967).

Renan, Ernest — Mission de Phénicie, (1864).

Bibliography (continued)

Salles, J-F.   La necrople "K" de Byblos,
                                (1982).

Save-Söderbergh, T.   Ägypten und Nubien (1941).

                                The Navy of the Eighteenth
                                Egyptian Dynasty of Egypt,
                                (1946).

Sethe, K.   "Der Name der Phönizier bei
                                Griechen und Ägyptern",
                                Mitteilungen der
                                Vorderasiatischen
                                Gesellschaft 21 (1917).

Simons, J.   The Geographical and
                                Topographical Texts of the
                                Old Testament, (1959).

Soyez, B.   Byblos et la Fête des Adonis
                                (1977).
Tufnell, O and
        Ward, W. A.   "Relations between Byblos,
                                Egypt and Mesopotamia at the
                                End of the Third Millennium
                                B.C.", Syria XLIII (1966).

Vandersleyen, C.   Les guerres d'Amosis, (1971).

Vercoutter, J.   L'Egypte et le monde égéen
                                préhellénique, (1956).

Ward, William A.   "Relations Between Egypt and
                                Mesopotamia from Prehistoric
                                Times to the End of the Middle
                                Kingdom". Journal of Economic
                                and Social History of the
                                Orient VII, Parts I and 2,
                                (1964), 1-45, 121-135.

Watson, Patty Jo   "The Chronology of North
                                Syria and North Mesopotamia
                                from 10,000 B.C. to 2000
                                B.C." in Robert W. Ehrich
                                (ed.), Chronologies in Old
                                World Archaeology, (1954).

Weill, Raymond   Phoenicia and Western Asia
                                to the Macedonian Conquest,
                                (1940).

Bibliography (continued)

Weissbach, F. H.   Die Denkmäler und Inschriften an der Mündung des Nahr el Kelb, (1922).

Zibelius, K.   Afrikanische   Orts-und Völkernamen, (1972).

Ägyptische Siedlungen nach Texten des alten Reiches, (1978).

LIST OF ABBREVIATIONS

AESEN   A. Nibbi, *Ancient Egypt and Some Eastern Neighbours* (1981).

AEO   A. H. Gardiner, *Ancient Egyptian Onomastica* 2 vols.

AfO   *Archiv für Orientforschung.*

Ann. Serv.   *Annales du Service des Antiquités de l'Egypte.*

AO   *Der Alte Orient.*

BASOR   *Bulletin of American Schools of Oriental Research.*

Beziehungen   W. Helck, *Beziehungen Ägyptens zu Vorderasien* (1962 and 1971).

BIFAO   *Bulletin de l'Institut Français d'Archéologie Orientale.*

Bi. Or.   *Bibliotheca Orientalis.*

Chr. d'Eg.   *Chronique d'Egypte.*

Couyat et Montet   J. Couyat et P. Montet, *Les inscriptions hiéroglyphiques et hiératiques du Ouadi Hammamat Mem. Inst. Fr. Or.* 34 (1912).

GM   *Göttinger Miszellen.*

IEJ   *Israel Exploration Journal.*

List of Abbreviations (continued)

IFAO
Institut français d'archéologie orientale.

JARCE
Journal of the American Research Center in Egypt.

JEA
Journal of Egyptian Archaeology.

JEOL
Jaarbericht Vooraziatisch-Egyptisch Gezelschap "Ex Oriente Lux".

JESHO
Journal of the Economic and Social History of the Orient.

JNES
Journal of Near Eastern Studies.

KRI
K. A. Kitchen, Ramesside Inscriptions.

Lexikon
W. Helck and E. Otto, Lexikon der Ägyptologie.

MDIAK
Mitteilungen des deutschen Instituts für ägyptische Altertumskunde in Kairo.

Medinet Habu
The Oriental Institute, The University of Chicago, Medinet Habu.

MIO
Mitteilungen des Instituts für Orientforschung.

MM
Mariner's Mirror.

MVAG
Mitteilungen der vorderasiatishen-ägyptischen Gesellschaft.

124

List of Abbreviations (continued)

OLZ   Orientalistische Literaturzeitung.

Orientalia   Commentarii editi dal Pontificio
               Istituto Biblico.

PEQ   Palestine Exploration Quarterly.

PM   B. Porter, R. Moss and J. Málék,
               Topographical Bibliography of Ancient
               Egyptian Hieroglyphic Texts, Reliefs
               and Paintings.

R d'E.   Revue d'Egyptologie.

Rec. Trav.   Recueil de travaux relatifs à la
               philologie et à l'archéologie
               égyptiennes et assyriennes.

SAK   Studien zur altägyptischen Kultur.

SPE   A. Nibbi, The Sea Peoples and Egypt
               (1975).

SPRES   A. Nibbi, The Sea Peoples: A
               Re-Examination of the Egyptian Sources
               (1972).

Urk. I   K. Sethe, Urkunden des Alten Reiches
               (1903).

Urk. IV   K. Sethe, Urkunden des 18. Dynastie
               (1927-30).

Wörterbuch   A. Erman and H. Grapow, Wörterbuch der
               ägyptischen Sprache (1926-31).

List of Abbreviations (continued)

ZAS   Zeitschrift für ägyptische Sprache und
                       Altertumskunde.

ZDMG   Zeitschrift   des   deutschen
                       morgenländischen Gesellschaft.

a

b

FIG. 15

PLATE VIII

PLATE IX

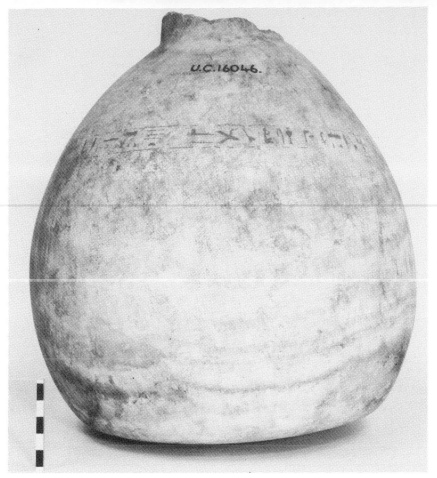

PLATE Xa

PLATE Xb

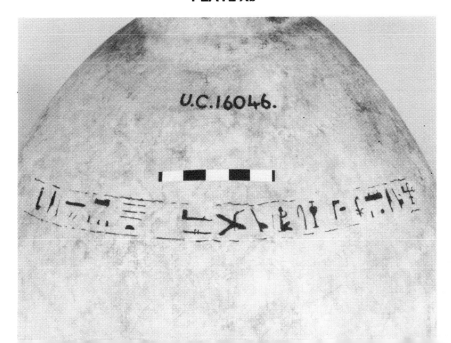

Printed for DE Publications, 13 Lovelace Rd., Oxford,
OX2 8LP, by Bocardo Press, Cowley, Oxford OX4 2EY.